How to Talk to Your Pets

Animal Communication for Dogs, Cats, & Other Critters

Gail Thackray

Printed in the United States of America
Thackray, Gail
    How To Talk To Your Pets: Animal Communication For Dogs, Cats & Other Critters / by Gail Thackray

ISBN-10: 098484404X
ISBN-13: 978-0-9848440-4-3

Project Consultant, Mara Krausz
Illustrations by Rachel Harris
Cover and layout design by Teagarden Designs
Cover photographs by Kevin Ellsworth

Published by
Indian Springs Publishing
P.O. Box 286
La Cañada, CA 91012
www.indianspringspublishing.com

Table Of Contents

Dedicated to all animals everywhere. If we could only return the love and respect they selflessly give us, the world would be a much better place. A portion of the profits from this book will go to help animals in need.

Most often a person who takes care of a pet is called an owner. If you are reading this book, you will probably agree with me that this term doesn't really encompass the relationship at all. You may think of yourself as guardian, parent, or partner. Perhaps you say that you are your animal's person.

Our animals often call us mom or dad. If they are closest to a child in the family, this child may be their mom or dad, or perhaps their sister or brother. Sometimes our pet may simply call us by our name. But for an animal to say, "my owner," it would be rare. And certain cats (you'll know if you have one) might think it's the other way around; that they own you! Still, it was hard to write using parent or guardian, so I hope you will forgive me when I write "owner." Just know that I mean the loving, caring guardian who is blessed to be partners with this wonderful creature.

CHAPTER 1

We Can All Do It!

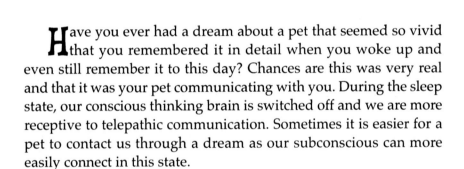

Have you ever had a dream about a pet that seemed so vivid that you remembered it in detail when you woke up and even still remember it to this day? Chances are this was very real and that it was your pet communicating with you. During the sleep state, our conscious thinking brain is switched off and we are more receptive to telepathic communication. Sometimes it is easier for a pet to contact us through a dream as our subconscious can more easily connect in this state.

Born to Communicate

We are all natural-born animal communicators. Unfortunately, we are taught from a very young age that it is not only impossible to talk to animals but that we are weird or abnormal if we say we can. So most of us block this wonderful natural ability, no longer able to even remember that we can communicate with other species.

Even though most people don't believe that they can talk to animals, many animal lovers will say they have a special relationship with their pet and that they somehow just know what their animal wants or when something is wrong with them. Some will even swear that their pet can understand what they say to them, as their pet reacted in such a way that this seems to be the only explanation.

Have you ever had your pet show up at the doorstep before you even called them? Has your cat hidden from you the very morning you had a veterinary appointment, as if he knew where he was going? Perhaps you've had an animal act strangely around a person that you feel uncomfortable with. Our pets can "hear" everything we say, whether we say it out loud or just in our head. They are constantly listening to us through the images, thoughts, and feelings we project. We are the ones who cannot hear them back. Actually we really can hear them, if we just know how to listen.

We Tend to Block Non-Verbal Communication

We all have this ability to be receptive to our surroundings. It's just that some of us block it more than others. We have become so busy with our lives, families, and careers that we often don't take the time to stop and listen to the more subtle messages of the Universe. It's like we have switched off this mode, as it interferes with whatever we are doing at the moment. Our lives have become too fast-paced to stop and allow. I have found that I need to take time to stop and relax and to get into the "mode" before communicating with an animal. I have to make a conscious effort to "switch on" as it were. The rest of the day, I am "switched off" and not paying as much attention to my intuition.

With all our modern forms of communication: cell phones, the Internet, texting, email, posting, etc, we've forgotten the little subtleties of one-on-one communication. A bombardment of fast, multiple forms of communication, along with the perceived necessity of multitasking, has become the norm. Much of our basic instinct to communicate through feelings, intuition, and other sensitivities has become suppressed. These other forms have taken a backseat and have been devalued.

Packets of Information

Animals communicate not only with their own species but with all species by using telepathic imagery. That is they are sending "packets" of their own thoughts and emotions to other animals. Yes they communicate with language (barks, chirps, etc.), but the more in-depth conversations take place on a higher consciousness level. Here they are able to easily and instantaneously transmit memories or thought packets from one to another. These thought packets contain visual moving images, the backstory or history, emotional feelings, and sensory imagery (e.g., smell, taste). It is as if they are downloading a memory "packet" to the receiver.

I believe at one point in time, humans also communicated through this more efficient method. However, once language was developed humans became more dependent upon the spoken word and less on telepathic messages and imagery. Today most of us can only pick up on minimal aspects of body language and the perception of feelings that accompany communication through speech. Even then these feelings or sensory data may be overruled by the written or spoken word communicated. Sadly, we have lost this much deeper form of communication using visual images of memory, thoughts, and the accompanying feelings and senses. We've replaced it with a less efficient, more one-dimensional language.

Rekindling This Ability

The good news is that we can all learn to rekindle this ability and, through practice, can relearn how to use this long-forgotten skill. I am going to give you specific exercises that will get you into the feeling-sensitivity mode that will enable you to develop this form of communication. You will learn how to send and receive these thoughts in full with all of the senses involved.

Now I know some of you are thinking that you need to be born with a "gift" and that this is not a skill that can be developed. This is simply not true. I certainly wasn't born this way! I was forty when, quite by accident, I discovered that I was able to do this. For me it was something that had probably been there all my life, I had just never thought about it and certainly never tried.

You may think that this ability is something that you need to spend years developing. Yes, some people do develop this more and more over time and with practice. However, some people simply need to be shown that psychic door and they pick it up almost immediately. I teach animal communication workshops and almost everyone comes out amazed at what they accomplished. Some leave the workshop nearly ready to be professional animal communicators and others have seen little snippets that they will take away and develop. Almost without exception, my students are able to do this, at least on some level. Most are absolutely shocked by what they were able to do.

We Are All Psychic

I am convinced that anyone can do this. It's just a matter of believing that you can. You also need to be in a situation where you are able to "have a go" and take the opportunity to prove it to yourself. For some of you, it may come quickly and naturally as soon as you apply the tools that I give you. For others, it may take time, patience, and practice, like a voice that is rusty. You may have to retrain your instrument and keep trying.

Many of us have had little glimpses that we can do this. We've known instinctively what our pet needs. We know what things we should say to make them understand us. We've even experienced psychic premonitions or knowings in other areas of our life, but haven't paid much attention. This all comes from the same place. Whether we know when our little dog wants to be lifted onto the couch or we have a negative feeling about someone we just met, our psychic intuition and spiritual connection all come from the same place. Now we are going to learn to tap into that, to harness it and pay attention to it.

A World Where All Can Communicate

I believe that if everyone could understand the animal kingdom, this world would be a better place. For the sake of all animals everywhere, I write this book and pledge to help others learn this wonderful connection. I hope this book will not only give you the tools to get you started but also inspire you to perfect this wonderful language and to continue to spread the word to others.

I invite you on this ride with me. I promise that as you learn to communicate with animals, it will open up an entirely new world for you, not only in your daily life with your pets but in your understanding of your life, your career, your goals, and in a much broader sense, the purpose of your life.

Anyone can do this.
It's just a matter of believing that you can.

Communicating telepathically is a natural ability.
We just need to learn to stop blocking it.

Have you ever had a dream about your pet that seemed unusually vivid? Pets often communicate through dreams.

As you learn to communicate with animals,
it will open up an entirely new world for you.

CHAPTER 2

How I Started Talking to Animals

Iwasn't born an animal communicator with some "special talent." Just like most people, I had flashes of insight that I dismissed as my imagination. In fact, I considered myself pretty "normal." So as I share my personal journey, first discovering my psychic abilities at age forty, and then animal communication shortly thereafter, you may see that perhaps this skill is not something extraordinary, but rather something that you can do, too.

Born to Love Animals

Growing up in Yorkshire, North England, I developed a love of nature and all animals, especially horses. My father died when I was young, and my brother and I were raised by our mom. I was the only one who was horse crazy, though. Don't ask me where it came from, but the family was driven nuts by watching me practice my mounting technique on the garden wall or worse, in front of the television. My mom had no interest in horses, and I had to resort to using my own resources to fulfill my dreams.

My first ride was on the local preacher's donkey, "Honk the Donkey." I made a deal with the preacher that I could ride all I wanted in return for taking an interest in his bible class. Honk wasn't very cooperative and unfortunately, by that age, I had lost my innate animal communication abilities. I had to resort to donkey bribery. Honk would only go one way, toward the pasture where his eyes were focused on an attractive female donkey. All the jumps were set up in a line, facing his lady friend. After we ran the jumps, I would have to dismount, turn him around, and drag him back to the beginning.

Pretending to Be Psychic

I loved all animals, especially my dog Penny, but my mission in life at this young age was to rescue all the dogs and cats from the animal shelter as well as any strays in my neighborhood. Being an entrepreneurial nine year old, I corralled all my friends to participate in my monthly "Garden Parties" in aid of the local animal shelter. Garden parties consisted of garage sale items collected from the neighbors and several carnival games set up to entertain the youngsters on the block, many of whom were just my friends. I had the same role each time as Gypsy Rosalie. I decked out the garden shed like a spooky séance room. I dressed in garishly large hoop earrings (actually curtain rings), a couple of brightly colored headscarves, and used an upside-down fishbowl for my "crystal ball." Palm and crystal ball readings were around $1, all in aid of the animals.

My love of animals never waned. My mom let me keep the occasional stray kitten or lost dog, along with my rabbits, hamsters, and other little critters. At fourteen I went to work at a local veterinary office. I was sure this was going to be my profession from as far back as I could remember. Although at the age of four, I declared that I wanted to be a rag-and-bone man when I grew up so that I could have a horse. (In the UK rag-and-bone men sold unwanted household items to local merchants, sometimes off a cart pulled by a horse.) My family was relieved that I became a little more academically minded and decided to use my love of animals for a more prestigious career as a vet. I worked for the local vet all through high school and during my premed college courses.

Predictions Come True

Many years had gone by since my days of hosting garden parties when one day, I bumped into an old friend. She earnestly asked me if I could read her palm again. I laughed and told her that I'd just made that stuff up, that it was just a silly game to raise money for my animal charity. But my friend insisted that everything I had told her that day had come true: what her first car would be, what she would study, and specific changes in her life. I offered an explanation that maybe she had done those things because I had given her the suggestion and not the other way around. Although I had to admit to myself that it did seem a little odd, as many of the things that happened were totally out of her control.

This was only the beginning. After I bumped into five or more friends whose life path had also followed, in uncanny detail, what I told them in my childhood readings, I started to think that perhaps there was something in it. I was interested in spirituality and the psychic realm, and I believed that some people could predict the future. I just didn't believe I was particularly psychic.

An Interest in Spiritualism

When I was in my early teens, my occasional interest in the psychic realm took me to a local Spiritualist church. I dragged a friend along with me. It was this little chapel where we listened to hymns and prayers before the main feature of the night, my reason for being there, a visiting medium. We didn't know what to expect. The medium wandered around the room, picking out people and saying things like, "I have your uncle here who died of cancer" to which the person might say, "Yes! I recognize him. Thank you." Then the medium moved on to the next person, bringing in passed over family members and loved ones with a little description. Then he stopped at me and said, "I have a big black stallion in spirit for you." As we left that night my friend remarked to me, "Everyone else got a granddad or an auntie or someone and you get a horse! Typical!"

A Psychic Predicts My Future

When I was about fourteen years old, I went to a psychic fair and had a palm reading. The reader told me that within six years, I would be living in another country. I told her this couldn't be because I was planning to be a vet. (Actually, I was adamant that I would be a vet.) She told me that I wouldn't become a vet and that I would first travel, then put the science side of my mind aside, using the artistic side more. She said I would eventually become an author, have some kind of television show interviewing people, and that even celebrities would come to me for advice. Of course I dismissed all of this as ridiculous. She wasn't very good I thought.

A few years later I had missed one grade in my final exams, which was unheard of for me. This resulted in my only being offered a scholarship to Cambridge to study general medicine rather than veterinary medicine. Becoming a doctor rather than a veterinarian was not ok with me. (Crazy, I know, but I was devastated.) Meanwhile, a modeling job marked the beginning of the many travels the psychic had described.

Moving Across the Pond

I came to Los Angeles at age nineteen to model. I planned to return to the UK for university and kept my spot at Cambridge by taking a year out. I never did go back…. The rest is history.

Many years went by as I enjoyed being an entrepreneur and started several successful businesses. I continued to do some modeling and acting, although I wasn't particularly suited to these right-brain activities. I later did much better as a producer, behind the camera. For twenty years, I stayed busy with various businesses that I created. I seemed to have a knack for knowing exactly what would work and was often hired as a consultant. I was told that I always seemed to pick the "ace deal." Of course, I realize now that it was my intuition guiding me! Meanwhile, I had three beautiful girls who all needed lots of my attention.

My love of animals continued, of course. I was always surrounded by a constant flow of adopted dogs and cats. As soon as I arrived in Los Angeles, I made the L.A. Equestrian Center my second home. My first regular mount was a horse named Tennessee who was owned by Loretta Swit (who played "Hot Lips" Houlihan on the television show *M*A*S*H)*. In 1990, I moved to my very own ranch with room for horses, dogs, and everything else. Little did I realize that I had been chosen to live at this wonderful sanctuary by Native American spirits and was drawn there for a much larger purpose.

I continued to be interested in spiritual pursuits and would "know" things intuitively, but my business life was much more in the forefront of my mind. Children and horses took up whatever time I had left. It wasn't until I turned forty that I experienced a life-changing shift and truly discovered the psychic world. I've often wondered why I waited so long, but I now realize that it was all part of my spiritual growth. I needed to be immersed in the very practical business world with all its ups and downs and learning lessons for a reason. I needed to experience time being a mom and just life in general before I was ready for my new life.

Learning Reiki

Meanwhile, my Auntie Pauline back in England had gone through quite a life change of her own. She went from being an insurance adjuster and working in an office to becoming a Reiki Master and healer. She was teaching Reiki healing and working with hospice patients. On one of her visits to Los Angeles she announced that she would like to attune me to Reiki. Auntie Pauline declared that she knew I was psychic and that this attunement would enhance my abilities.

We spent a weekend at my ranch where she explained this ancient Japanese healing technique and then she attuned me to its energy. The attunement is like a ceremony where sacred Reiki symbols are passed to the person. I was expecting to feel something akin to a bolt of lighting going through me. I was a little disappointed to merely feel a little heat and tingling.

I didn't think a whole lot about it afterward. I did practice though, and the friends that received my healings swore they made a huge difference. Still, I wasn't very convinced.

My Awakening to the Spirit World

Shortly after this I heard about a weekend workshop on spirituality and mediumship given by a prominent English psychic, Angelica. I was intrigued, mostly because I was hoping for a reading from her as I had lost a friend recently and really wanted to reconnect with him. I talked my mom into joining me.

We started with an exercise where we were to imagine that a spirit belonging to someone else in the group was sitting next to us and that we could talk to them. Then we would get up in front of the group and share what we saw. The first person got up and said, "I think I see an old woman. She could be short but maybe tall and has an initial B or D or E...maybe." As the next few people got up, it was a similar guessing game. Even though what they were sensing was vague, what had my attention was that they seemed to actually be sensing someone next to them!

Then it was my turn. I was thinking that I'd done something wrong. I didn't "feel" anything. I couldn't sense anyone next to me. I was worried that I was about to look stupid. Unlike everyone else, I thought that what we were supposed to do was make up an imaginary story. Angelica encouraged me to just go for it and share what I got.

I looked directly at a guy in the group and said, "Mine is for you. I have Grand Pierre Marceau..." and I continued on to say how he died, what he did for a living, details of a photo, and a pressing message about a family business that had been dropped. After going on for a good five minutes, I stopped and said sheepishly, "Do you recognize any of that?" The guy's chin had hit the floor. "That was his name, that's what he did, I have that photo, everything you said is true!" He was shocked.

He was shocked! I just about freaked out! "How did I do that?!" I thought to myself. I continued throughout the weekend talking to everyone's relatives. When I went home that night, I couldn't sleep. It was as if a door had been opened and they were all lining up to chat. By the end of the workshop, I was freaked out, unnerved, exhausted, and my life had been changed forever....

I didn't immediately jump into a career as a psychic medium. Actually, it took about a year of practicing on friends to convince myself that this was even real. After all, I was very down-to-earth and business and science-oriented. If I couldn't prove it, it probably wasn't real, or so I thought.

My Animal Teachers

At this point I still had no idea that any of this related to animals. Then about six months later, I was browsing at a bookstore. There happened to be a lady giving a talk on animal communication. What a coincidence (as if there is such a thing!). I stayed and enjoyed the talk. Several people had booked a reading with the pet psychic after the talk and were waiting with photos of their pets in hand. Curious to see what I would pick up, I asked some of the guests if I could take a look at their pictures.

The first photo I looked at was that of a young dog. Immediately, I felt like I had stepped into the dog's body and was feeling his personality. "Tell them I am really good with the cats! You know most dogs would not be as good as me. I did take my bone behind the shed, though, just in case." I had a vision of two young kittens and digging a hole for my yellow rubber bone behind the garden shed. To my surprise the owners confirmed every detail.

Was this all in my mind or was it some kind of spiritual connection? Before I had time to analyze this, my thoughts jumped into the bodies of the two kittens. They were excitedly looking out the window at a large oak tree. From my point of view it had a huge trunk that towered high into the sky. I was feeling absolutely appalled and violated by what was going on outside my window. There was a whole bunch of pesky little squirrels running back and forth around the tree and even up and down it. "I need to get out. I need to do something about those critters," I thought. "I can't believe my dad is just allowing this! And the dog, he's not doing anything either! I need to get out and do something!!!"

When I asked the kittens what they were watching, I felt a more angelic persona come over me as they pleaded, "Ask our dad if we can PLEASEEEEE go outside. We'll be soooo good! I promise we will!" Apparently the dad would be on the porch every afternoon with his "dark liquid." (I thought cola, but it was actually beer.) The family had noticed the squirrels around the tree, but they had no idea that this was driving the kittens crazy.

I had come up with so many strange little details that I knew I couldn't be making it up. Plus the feeling that I was actually there in the bodies of such distinct personalities, I knew there had been a real connection.

In a strange way, connecting with animals seemed to be exactly the same process that I utilized to connect to spirits on the other side. Although now I was not only connecting to the other side, but also with those living and cross-species. All of this was just through a photograph! My psychic life was about to get a whole lot more interesting.

Going Professional

After this remarkable night I started practicing on friends. At every opportunity, I would ask if they had a photograph of one of their pets (one that I didn't know). They would often shriek in delight at things that I would pick up, but I am sure I was even more thrilled than they were. As a newly ordained medium, I was practicing on anyone who would let me, connecting with their loved ones in spirit, talking to their animals, and throwing in my Reiki healing. Sill, it was very much a hobby as I continued my busy life as a mom and businesswoman.

Eventually I was thrown into the deep end. As I got more entrenched in this new world, I decided to put on a psychic fair at my ranch. This involved bringing in all the psychic readers and animal communicators that I had made friends with, but certainly not me. I thought I wasn't ready for that. However, when I went to another fair in the hopes of promoting my own upcoming event, I somehow got roped into doing readings. The next thing I knew, they announced a lecture, "Gail Thackray on How to Communicate with Animals." This was the start of this wonderful journey that led to living my dream, teaching people over the world to communicate with animals, connect with their spirituality, and develop their own psychic abilities.

This ability to "talk" to animals gave me a whole new perspective on our furry friends: their unconditional love, their understanding of the cycle of life and death, and their unparalleled selfless devotion. At that moment I knew that this was not a gift simply given to me but an understanding that needs to be known by everyone. If I could teach others how to do this and each person could teach someone else, the planet would surely become a better place.

Not Born Psychic

So as you can see, I wasn't born a psychic. Although I always loved animals, I never thought that I could talk to them. I believed there were people who could talk to animals but that these "special" people were probably very sensitive and maybe even a little off-kilter from the rest of us. So what enabled me to suddenly be able to speak to spirits on the other side during that mediumship workshop? Was it my attunement to Reiki that opened me up? I am not sure, but it seems that it may have had something to do with my sudden psychic opening. Was this psychic ability there all along and I somehow managed to trick my mind into "having a go" or "making it up"? I am not completely sure, but as I continue to teach mediumship, developing intuition, and animal communication, I find some people, like me, open up in a big way instantly, while others develop their connection over time. What I have found for certain is that everyone is able to do this on some level and that once we tap into this world, it opens up our intuition in many other areas as well.

CHAPTER 3

The Purpose of Communication

The purpose of animal communication is to deepen your relationship with your animal friends and to forge a more meaningful partnership. It is not about controlling or training your pet. First and foremost, your intention for communication must be positive.

How Deep Is Our Connection?

Although many pet owners feel that they have a deep understanding of and a special connection with their beloved pet, their actual connection is so much deeper. If we can only break down our barriers, we will see just how intricate our relationships are and how much further our loving connection can go. You will be amazed to learn how much your furry friend knows about your life, not just in the home, but with your relationships and at work as well. They truly are our partners in life. Once you get a glimpse of what they really know and how deep their partnership with us truly is, it will surely give you a whole new perspective.

You may go into this thinking that animal communication is an interesting skill and it'll be fun to understand what your pets are thinking. Perhaps you even see this as a "party trick." However, as you read further and delve into this more, you will be amazed and in awe of what you can learn from the animal kingdom. You will be surprised at the breadth of knowledge and emotion that you will sense from them. I promise you that it will give you a whole new understanding of our place in the Universe.

Animal communication is not a training method nor does it have anything to do with understanding an animal's barks and tweets. It has to do with developing your spiritual instrument and opening up psychically so you can be more in tune with the animal kingdom and, in turn, your whole world.

As you experience talking with animals yourself, you will be amazed at these selfless, highly enlightened spirits that are more involved with us than you could ever imagine. Working with us as healing pets, protectors, teachers, and advisors, we can learn much from these wonderful creatures. Believe me, when you understand what you can learn through them, your entire outlook on life will drastically change.

Practical Applications for Animal Communication

There are many practical applications for animal communication that you will soon appreciate. Learning to communicate with your pet can transform your relationship, making it easier to modify unwanted behaviors, find out their likes and dislikes, and learn why they do the things that puzzle you. Discovering why an animal does something can be eye-opening. However, be forewarned. You may find out there is a message for you in their behavior! It may relate to what you are doing in your own life just as much as the behavior is some quirk in the pet's own personality.

Our pets come to us in many ways and we often don't know their history. Understanding where they came from and how this has shaped their personality can give you greater insight into why they act a certain way. Having this understanding and therefore being able to adapt for it may even help an owner to not give up an animal who may be aggressive or have other behavioral issues.

What about an animal that isn't housetrained or starts to chew your best shoes? Many unacceptable behaviors can be resolved when you know how to listen to your pet. We all know how frustrating it can be to not know what's wrong and never be able to make any headway in the process, especially when this is a loved pet that you couldn't bear to part with. Having a skill to help solve this issue with your animal partner can be a blessing. Many times the root cause turns out to be something that the owner is doing inadvertently and can quickly be resolved.

Having an animal is a life decision and not to be taken lightly. Being in tune with the animal species can help you to select a pet that is right for you, one that will be a good partner and will fit in with the rest of your family.

Understanding an animal's health and physical condition can save you from distress and heartache as well as potential vet bills or even losing a loved pet. The skill of telepathic communication will help you determine how best to keep your pet in optimal health and help you to work better with your veterinarian.

When a pet has got lost or run away, it can be a frantic, devastating event for the owner who loves them dearly. Learning animal communication gives you the skills that may help you connect to your pet and then help to guide them home.

Animals in Spirit and in Transition

For those of us who have loved a pet who has passed into spirit, you know this can be as devastating as losing a human member of the family. Animals are our loves, our lives, and yet we feel so helpless when their time has come. What if we could understand death, the process of passing over, and where our pets go? This, I am sure, would give great comfort to any pet owner.

Sometimes our animals are hanging on just for us. Other times it is their time to go and no matter what we do to help them, they will pass. At times there may be something we can do to help them, to ease the process, or even extend their time here on earth. What animal lover would not want this knowledge, this ability to be more connected with their pet through their last days? To those who have lost a dear friend who is now in spirit, wouldn't it be a wonderful gift to be able to hear from them again? What if you could reconnect, share the love, and know where they are and what they are doing? We may wonder if we will ever be together again physically. I can tell you this, many animals follow us through our lives, reincarnating several times during our lifetime. How will we know if they will come back and how will we recognize them?

Our Pets Are Our Partners

Most surprising of all, I have learned through my many sessions that often our animals see us as not only their family, but they have a purpose with us or a job in our life. Sometimes that job is to be our partner. I am not just talking about bringing us love and support, which they surely do, but I am talking about actually being our supportive partner. I have found animals that act as healers, helping to heal us and also helping us to heal others. I've talked to animals that help with our creative lives by relaying specific information to us that we presume is our own intuition or creative imagination. Animals direct us in all aspects of our lives and careers, working alongside us and passing along thoughts that we believe are our own. What if you could truly communicate with your animal partner?

A Spiritual Connection

Animals have access to a kind of shared cosmic knowledge, so in their higher consciousness, they are able to draw on this knowledge and assist in a manner that is difficult for us to comprehend. Their emotional depth is far deeper than anything we understand and their unconditional love provides a selfless example we could all learn from.

As you work on your ability to sense and communicate telepathically, you are working on your spirituality. Although animal communication may be your primary interest, you will find that as you redevelop this skill (a skill that we all inherently have and have just forgotten how to use), you are elevating your spiritual self and you will become more enlightened in many other areas of your life. As you learn to connect to animals and develop your psychic senses, you also open up your connection to the spirit world and perhaps to mediumship. After learning to communicate with animals, some people also discover that they can similarly talk to loved ones who have passed.

What You Will Learn

Learning to communicate with animals will take you on an extraordinary journey and give you the skill set to:

* ❖ Not only improve the life of your animal but also your own.
* ❖ Discover your pet's history and the shaping of its behaviors.
* ❖ Understand your pet's likes and dislikes.
* ❖ Choose the right pet for you.
* ❖ Understand your pet's health and aid them to be in optimal health.
* ❖ Locate a missing animal.
* ❖ Negotiate with your pet to modify behaviors.
* ❖ Understand the process of death and know when to let go.
* ❖ Connect to animals on the other side.

CHAPTER 4

Connecting with Your Animal Guides

I believe that we all have human spirit guides as well as animal guides. Our animal guide could be a wild animal, Native American Power Animal, or even a mythological creature. Sometimes they are domestic animals such as a dog or cat, or a pet of ours who has passed over. Often these animal guides will help us to connect in animal communication. We are going to do a meditation to meet one of your animal guides.

Meditation to Meet Your Animal Guide

Before you do any work in the psychic realm, including meditation, always protect yourself. The following is a simple protection technique that I personally use.

Visualize a bright star in the sky and this star's white rays of light are beaming down over the top of your head. Imagine this white healing light coming down over your shoulders, slowly down over your torso, and then completely enveloping your entire body in pure white light in the highest of goodness. You are now protected in this bubble of white light energy and only good energies can come into your aura.

Now you are ready for the meditation. (You may want a friend to read this aloud to you during or familiarize yourself with it first so that you will not need to look at your book while you are meditating.)

Sitting comfortably, place your hands on your lap with your palms facing up. Concentrate on your breathing, taking a deep breath in from your nose, holding it for a second, and then breathing out long and forcefully through your mouth. With each breath out, envision releasing negative energy and relaxing deeper and deeper.

Imagine that you are in a cottage in the woods. You wake up and open the door. It is a beautiful morning. The birds are singing and the sun is shining down on you. You decide to walk out of the cottage and go down a footpath through the woods. The sun is warm on your neck but not too hot. It is a beautiful day and you are surrounded by nature. Take a moment to appreciate this scene of magnificent beauty.

As you walk down this path, you see a clearing in the woods ahead. As you approach the middle of this clearing, you see a bubbling brook. Along the bank of this brook you see an old oak tree. Sit underneath this tree for a moment and listen to the sounds of the rushing water.

As you sit by the brook appreciating its beauty, ask that your animal spirit guide come sit beside you. Let an animal appear to you and gently encourage him or her to come close. This may be a pet that you had that is now in spirit and looking after you as your animal guide or it may be an animal who you are not familiar with. It may be a domestic, wild, or mythological animal.

Look into their eyes and thank them for being your animal spirit guide. Take a moment to reconnect and to share the love you have always had together. Thank them for being your animal spirit guide. Ask if they have a message for you at this time in your life and take a moment to listen for an answer.

If you have a question for your animal spirit guide, ask if it is ok to ask your question at this time. If you wish to be reacquainted with a loved one (person or pet) who has passed, ask if they can bring them forth.

Repeat this affirmation: I am able to connect and communicate with animals. My heart is open and I am able to receive messages from them. I relax in knowing that you, my animal spirit guide, are with me during my communication and I know that you will help me to understand the messages clearly.

End by thanking your animal spirit guide for being with you. Say goodbye for now. Know that your animal spirit guide remains close by you throughout your life and that you can come to this special place again and speak with them.

Ask that when you remember this special place, you will be put back in touch with both this place and with your animal guide. Imagine leaving your special place and walking back down the path to the cottage.

You are now sitting in a chair in the cottage. Then slowly see yourself back in your own room. Imagine a white light going down through your spine to the ground, keeping you firmly grounded in this world. When you awaken, you will feel refreshed and ready to take on your life challenges, knowing that your animal spirit guide is always with you.

Now slowly open your eyes and know that you can always call on your animal spirit guide.

What animal guide came to you during your meditation? Did this make sense to you? It is not unusual to find that your animal guide is an animal you feel a close kinship to. You may have a similar pet, artwork, memorabilia, or photographs of this animal. For instance, a person with a tiger for a guide may be intrigued by safaris, dream of taking a trip to India, or wear tiger print clothing. A person with an elephant guide may have a collection of elephant statues at home, and a person with bird spirit guide may find that the wild birds in their neighborhood like to be in their yard.

If you are doing this meditation with a group, before starting it might be interesting to see what animal the other group members associate with you. It is entertaining to see that we can often guess a person's animal spirit guide based on their personality. For instance, someone who has a deer as a guide might be a shy, cautious person whereas someone who has a lion may have a proud and strong personality. A person who has a horse as a spirit guide may have an adventurous spirit but likes to return to their family, as horses are inherently pack animals.

Some people will see one main animal guide and others will see a few different ones. Most of the time people can relate to the animals they meet in meditation and, on occasion, they are blown away because of the strong connection they already have with that animal. The recognition and confirmation of this connection can be momentous.

What kind of animals do you display in your life
(e.g., through clothing, art, photos)?

Do you collect animal figurines or artwork?

What animals resonate with you?

What animals do you love?

Animal spirit guides can be:

Domestic animals

Your own pets who have passed over

Wild animals

Native American Power Animals

Mythological creatures (e.g., dragon, unicorn)

CHAPTER 5

Preparation Exercises

It is very difficult to switch off our active, thinking brain that wants to learn how to communicate and instead access our subconscious mind that simply allows. This is the key to successful communication. The following practice exercises will help us to do this.

We often put high expectations on ourselves, expecting to be able to master a new skill immediately otherwise we feel that we've somehow failed. In my workshops, I tell people not to compare themselves with others. Trying too hard can inadvertently block your psychic flow. Don't question or analyze the exercises, simply follow these practice exercises and don't overthink them. Just go with the flow.

Exercise - Pretending

This is an exercise to practice using your imagination. There is no animal communication required here–so don't feel pressured. Allow yourself to creatively pretend. Use your imagination and make things up.

First imagine a dog in the room. Create this dog in your imagination. Be sure it is one that you don't know. I want you to create this in as much detail as possible: the breed, age, personality, likes and dislikes, etc. Now imagine being inside the body of that dog. How does it feel? Are you old and tired? Grumpy? Or are you a young excited pup? Feel your body. Feel your tail.

Now someone is rolling a ball back and forth, playing with you. As the dog, how do you feel about the ball and the game? Are you excited? Or are you totally disinterested? Imagine playing a game with the ball or simply ignoring it.

Now glance up at the refrigerator. You see a cat perched on the top. How do you feel about the cat? Now take yourself out of the body of the dog and transform yourself into the cat. You are looking down at the dog with the ball. How do you feel about that dog? How do you feel about the scene that you are watching? Do you know the dog? Are you afraid of the dog? Do you have an opinion about the dog playing with the ball? How does it feel to be perched up high looking down? What does it feel like to be inside the cat? What is your personality as the cat? What breed of cat are you? What does your body feel like?

As the cat you glance at the other side of the room and notice a bird in a cage. How do you feel about this? What do you think about the bird? Now leave the body of the cat and jump inside the body of the bird. As the bird you see the cat as well as the dog with the ball. You are looking over the scene. How do you feel about each of them and their being in the room with you? Do you like your cage? Is the door to your cage open or closed? Does it make you feel safe or does it make you feel constrained? What does it feel like to be the bird?

Now go back into your own body with your feet on the floor. Feel your fingers, toes, and your bottom in the chair. Feel yourself physically planted in your body and grounded again.

What did this experience feel like? What impressions did you get? There are no right or wrong answers. This is simply your imagination at work and the idea is to feel your imagination at play and in as great detail as possible.

How does it feel to use your imagination? This is the same feeling that you will have about animal communication at first. If your telepathic communication is not flowing, start by using your own imagination and then allowing the animal's energy to jump in. If you ask an animal their favorite food and you don't get anything at first, just imagine it. Imagine the bowl and then what is in that bowl. You may turn out to be exactly right. Perhaps you decide to imagine dog bone treats in the bowl and then a thought suddenly replaces the treats with a slice of pizza. This is an example of kick-starting your creative juices yourself and then the dog will use your imaginary channel to interject their thoughts.

There is only a subtle difference between the feeling of imagining and the feeling of telepathic communication. This is because it is through your own thought channel that the animal's thoughts come. Don't be afraid to use your imagination.

Exercise - Pretending

- ❖ You are the dog playing with the ball.

- ❖ You are the cat looking at the dog.

- ❖ You are the cat looking at the bird.

- ❖ You are the bird looking at the cat and the dog.

Exercise - Passing Feelings

We are constantly picking up on other people's feelings and energy without even realizing it. I use this exercise to show people just how psychically sensitive they already are.

First pair up with a partner. One person agrees to be the sender and the other is the receiver (afterwards we switch). Find a friend who will be open to doing this exercise with you.

Sit facing your partner. Before you begin, each of you should do a white light of protection visualization because you will be opening up psychically. The sender is instructed to think of the feeling of love and then to put this feeling into a shape. It can be any shape, three-dimensional or flat, simple or complex. For example, it could be a heart, square, ball, pyramid, etc. The sender is then asked to give this shape containing this love a color. It can be a simple color or hue. It can also be rainbow or perhaps it is pink with white dots. Then the sender is asked to give this colored shape a smell. It can be anything. Examples may be anywhere from floral or fruity to baking smells like cinnamon or chocolate or various other scents.

As the sender creates all of this in their imagination, they continue to go over in their mind: the color, shape, scent, and the feeling of love. They then choose an animal to deliver this message of love along with the shape, color, and scent. The sender imagines this animal passing this shape and its attributes to the receiver. The receiver is to allow these images to flow to them. As they allow the thoughts and feelings to wash over them, they are to pay particular attention to all of their senses.

After allowing the passing and receiving for a few minutes, both parties pull back into their physical body and return to the physical world. The receiver is then asked to reveal what they received. Did they guess the correct shape, color, scent, and animal? You will be surprised at the accuracy. Maybe you won't get everything correct, but you may get some things very close or even exact. I'm always amazed by how many people are able to sense many of the elements being sent. I've even seen the sender pick an attribute and then switch it in their mind just as they are sending it and the recipient picks up on both choices!

Sometimes rather than picking up both choices, having more than one thing in your mind when you send the information inadvertently clouds things. The receiver may get both choices, but they also pick up on the indecision and it becomes confusing. Even though you would assume that it is easier to send than receive, you see that it is not as easy to send a message as one might think. You need to be clear in your choice of what you are sending and be careful that you are not sending mixed messages. Now you can see how sometimes you could be sending a confusing message to your pet.

Exercise - Passing Feelings

- ❄ Think about the feeling of love.

- ❄ Give it a shape.

- ❄ Give it a color.

- ❄ Give it a smell.

- ❄ Choose an animal to pass this feeling and its attributes to the receiver.

Exercise - Passing Energy

Another exercise I use in my workshops that is similar to passing feelings is passing energy using a stuffed animal. Everyone pairs up again and each person should have a stuffed animal. Concentrate on your stuffed animal, giving it an imaginary personality, favorite food, and a favorite activity. As you hold it between your hands, project the feeling of each item into your stuffed animal. Afterward, swap with your partner. You are going to try to sense the attributes that were placed into your partner's stuffed animal. Can you sense the personality, favorite food, and favorite activity it was imbued with? When you are asked, for example, to say the personality trait you picked up on, just relax and blurt out the first thing that comes to mind.

Once again, you may be amazed by how accurate you are in reading the energy that was put into the stuffed animal by your partner. Our thoughts and feelings have energy. This is an example of how we can project our energy into an inanimate object and how others can pick up on this energy.

Exercise - Passing Energy

- ❄ Use a stuffed animal.

- ❄ Give it a personality.

- ❄ Give it a favorite food.

- ❄ Give it a favorite activity.

CHAPTER 6

10 Steps to Connect

In this chapter I am going to teach you the basic skills of connecting and communicating with an animal. You may have thought that there is some complex language to learn or an elaborately structured activity to do. Actually it is far more basic which, unfortunately, makes it a lot more unbelievable to most people. In fact, all we are trying to accomplish is to remove the barrier we have had all our life that says, "This is impossible. I can't do this." Communication with animals or with anyone telepathically is not difficult, strenuous, or anything that you need to work on. It is simply a way of being, a way of allowing that we normally prevent ourselves from accepting.

Meditating and doing the exercises in Chapter 5 will help you to step back from your thinking brain and allow you to just be. This will allow you to tap into and receive this wonderful gift you already have. Rather than learning a whole new skill, I am showing you how to experience what you already know deep in your subconscious.

Use a Photograph of an Animal You Don't Know

I suggest that your first subject be a type of animal that you are most familiar with, like a dog or cat. It should be an animal that you don't know and it is preferable that the owner is there with you so they can verify the details you are receiving. This helps you to gauge if you are connected. The photo can be of an animal who is alive or passed on, it doesn't matter at this point and the owner doesn't need to tell you. In my workshops we pair up and swap photos of our pets.

A photo works just as well or better than being face to face with the animal. It may even be easier because you won't be distracted by any personality traits that you observe or may assume from seeing the animal in person. If you can get a photo with the animal's eyes clearly visible, this is best as the eyes really are the windows to the soul. If not, any picture should still work ok.

Practicing often with photos is a great training tool. Perhaps you can bring together a group of friends who wish to learn animal communication and everyone can swap photos. I have also included some practice photos at the back of this book.

After we have learned to connect with an animal through a photograph, we can move on to in-person animals. Eventually you will be able to tap in and connect with an animal without either a photo or them being present. You'll be able to do this just by thinking of them.

Once you have built up confidence in your ability to communicate with other people's pets, you can start to communicate with your own animals. The reason to start with another person's pet is because you have preconceived ideas about what your own pet would say. Since you know your own animals so well, it is difficult to decipher what you are receiving from your animal from what is wishful thinking or an assumption based on what you know of their personality. Once you are successful at receiving information from an animal who you don't know and are able to verify this information with their owner, then you can communicate with confidence with your own animal. Eventually you will get to the point where you don't need that validation because you will have learned to trust in your communication skills.

The 10 Basic Steps

These are the 10 basic steps you will be using to connect. A more detailed description follows. Find a quiet place where you will not be disturbed. Be sure that you have enough time so that you can be completely relaxed and not feel rushed.

Step 1 - Protect Yourself Psychically

In any psychic or meditative work where you are opening yourself to other realms, you must first protect yourself. I like to protect myself with white light.

Step 2 - Get in the Communicating Zone

You are going to get into a "communicating zone" through meditation, which raises your vibration and allows you to be more sensitive psychically.

Step 3 - Call in Your Animal Guides

You are going to call in your guides, especially your animal spirit guides, to help you connect to the animal and to assist you in understanding the messages.

Step 4 - Connect to the Animal

Look at the photo. Especially study their eyes. Send the animal love, appreciation, and gratitude. Ask for their permission to connect. (If the animal is present, either look or imagine looking into their eyes.)

Step 5 - Heart-to-Heart Connection

Imagine sending the animal love directly from your Heart Chakra to theirs. Then imagine receiving love back from their Heart Chakra to yours.

Step 6 - Start with Simple Questions

Start with simple, small talk questions for verification. As you get a sense of the animal's personality, you are allowing the connection to strengthen.

Step 7 - Listen with Imagination and Heart

Allow your imagination to flow. Let thoughts drift into your head and the feelings to wash over you.

Step 8 - Ask More Important Questions

Now that you have asked several simple questions and received verification, go on to questions about behavior, health, and other issues.

Step 9 - End Your Session. Thank the Animal

Don't forget to thank the animal and to honor (or have the owner honor) any promises you made during the session.

Step 10 - Disconnect Your Energy

Disconnect yourself psychically. Protect again and ground yourself.

Remember–If at first you don't succeed, take a break, and then try again.

Find a Quiet Place and Make Time

It's a busy day. I have to pick up kids, run to the store, and do my usual multi-tasking along the way. As I arrive home frazzled, I have a message on my desk. It reads, "Don't forget to call Diane about her dog and you have a reading at 4 PM with a lady about her cat (you said you were free for a couple of hours)." Oh sure, I have time.... Unfortunately my subconscious self doesn't have time!

At first this was how I tried to do my work, but I soon realized that this is not an ability that you can switch on and off instantaneously. It is nearly impossible for me to be busy with life and using my left brain, and then suddenly switch to this very creative right-brain functioning. I have found that I often need at least an hour to just unwind from the day before I can get into the communication zone and there is no way this process can be rushed.

I'm sure some people can switch on more quickly than I or already exist in a constant right-brain creative mood. For me, I can no more communicate with animals when I'm rushed than I can be in a romantic mood after a heated conversation. Neither could I write poetry or sketch a beautiful picture in between business meetings. You need to block out time and never rush yourself. The process will get quicker, but at first you need the time to decompress from whatever else is going on in your life.

First find a place where you won't be disturbed, one that feels comfortable and safe to you. It may be outside in the garden or a favorite place that you have. Maybe it is your bedroom or another quiet area of the house. This place should also be a comfortable location for you to sit. It is better to not lie in bed as you may get too cozy and fall asleep.

Sit comfortably to begin. I like to sit with my feet uncrossed and my palms resting on my lap, facing up toward the ceiling. Crossing your arms and legs can block your energy and stop the creative flow. Most importantly, you need to feel comfortable.

In preparing to communicate with an animal, we are going through many of the same techniques you may see recommended for meditation. It is the same "zone" I get into to communicate with loved ones who have passed over or to do an energy healing. We are simply aligning ourselves with the natural energy of the Universe or Divine Source.

Step 1 – Protect Yourself Psychically

Before you start any psychic work or meditation, it is very important to protect yourself. Do not skip this part.

If you believe in God, Jesus, Buddha, or some other deity who helps you to feel protected, ask them to be with you. Ask to be encompassed by their love, that they surround you and protect you from any negative influences.

I personally ask God for protection. I then imagine a bright star in the sky shining down on me, giving off a white light that is radiating down over me. As this white light comes over my body, I feel that it is the love and protection of God. I imagine this white light as it completely engulfs my body. I ask that only good energies from the highest of goodness be in my aura and that I will be protected from any lower vibrational energies.

I am sometimes asked if animal communication is somewhat ungodly or anti-Christian. It is none of these. However, we are opening ourselves up to other realms to communicate. In doing so, we are open to receiving messages, emotions, and connection from spiritual sources. Just as there are positive light energies, there are lower vibrational influences around us. It is best to protect ourselves so that only the highest vibrations will be around us.

Step 2 – Get in the Communicating Zone

Take a few deep breaths, being conscious of the sound of your breath. As you inhale, imagine that positive energy is coming into your lungs and as you exhale, imagine all the stresses and negative energy leaving your body. You can continue to concentrate on your breathing if this helps you to relax.

You are decompressing from your daily life, releasing all your worries and stresses. Tell yourself that everything is on hold for the next hour and that you are only going to concentrate on your inner self and well-being.

Imagine a white light coming down over your head. As it passes over your shoulders, imagine your shoulder muscles relaxing and blood flowing easily through all your veins and arteries, creating balanced energy around your shoulders. Imagine this happening to each part of your body as the light shines down over each area until your entire body is relaxed. Imagine this white light radiating down over you until it completely engulfs your body. See it wrapping around your toes and placing you in a bubble of light. As you do this, imagine this light clearing out any negativity and creating a state of well-being in your body. Energy is circulating through your entire body and you feel in optimal health. Your busy thoughts slowly disappear as your mind quiets.

Now I want you to imagine a wonderful place where you feel

comfortable, happy, and at peace. This could be a place you wish to go or somewhere you've already been. It could be a memory of a vacation or a completely imaginary scene. Perhaps you are on a tropical beach sitting under a palm tree listening to the waves gently rolling over your toes. Or perhaps you are sitting in your garden listening to the birds chirping. It could be a memory of holding a newborn baby.

Your vision can change midstream as you allow your thoughts to wander. This doesn't have to be your best fantasy or your most favorite place. I don't want you to keep switching as you try to find the "best" scenario, just settle on a place that gives you a nice warm fuzzy feeling. Also, do not use an image of a person or animal whom you have loved and lost. Even though this may bring a happy sensation, it will have some sad feelings mixed in as well. Just find something that makes you feel good and don't over complicate it. There is no right or wrong.

Once you have found your paradise for the moment, hold that vision and soak in the wonderful warm feeling that it gives you. Feel appreciation for how wonderful you feel in this place, whether it is for the birds singing, the natural beauty, or the clouds that feel like pillows. Sit in appreciation for a minute. Be still and quiet, aware of your surroundings. Notice the noises, smells, and sensations. Once you feel completely relaxed and in a state of peace, move on to the next step.

Step 3 – Call in Your Animal Guides

You are going to ask your animal spirit guide to accompany you. Your spirit guides, both human and animal, are always helping you whether you realize it or not. You will now acknowledge your animal guide working with you and helping you to communicate today.

While you are still imagining being in your wonderful place, ask your animal spirit guide to come sit beside you. Look in front of you and to your right. In the distance, imagine an animal coming toward you. This animal only comes in love so do not be afraid. (An animal spirit guide will never cause harm.) Ask this animal to come and sit down beside you. They usually sit to your right as the right side represents the emotional and spiritual side of you. It will likely be an animal you have never met, perhaps a wild animal or even a fictional animal. Although it could also be a pet you have loved and lost. You may be surprised. Just allow whatever comes to you and try not to direct the scene.

This is going to be your animal guide for your communication today or perhaps this animal will always appear for you. Thank your animal guide for coming and for helping you. Imagine love going out from your heart to their heart. Imagine your breathing is in sync and with each breath, love passes between the two of you. Your animal guide is going to sit quietly to your right and they will be there to aid you with the communication.

Now keeping that relaxed and loving feeling with your animal guide, we are going to try to connect to your animal subject.

Step 4 – Connect to the Animal

Look at the photo of the animal. Look deep into their eyes. As you do this, allow yourself to feel almost mesmerized or in a semi-trance-like state.

Then very gently and lovingly, in your imagination, ask the animal for permission to connect. Just as in life, if you were to walk up to an animal that you didn't know, you would not brusquely shove your hand in their face. You would bend down to their level and gently put out your hand, inviting them to come to sniff it. Imagine this soft, gentle invitation. When you've connected, you will feel an acknowledgement. It will feel like love and acceptance. A "yes" may be heard in your mind, but you may also simply feel a loving connection. You may be aware of emotions or feelings that do not seem to be yours. Very rarely will you get a "no." If you do get a "no," just respect it for now. You can always try again later.

Step 5 – Heart-to-Heart Connection

As you look deeply into their eyes, allow yourself to sink into your heart and feel love. Send the animal love and appreciation. Feel with your heart and consciously send love to them. Imagine sending love directly from your Heart Chakra to theirs. Then imagine receiving love back from their Heart Chakra to yours.

Animals work in the energy of love. You are allowing yourself to communicate through love. Now all of your intentions and communications come with love. With each breath out, send your animal love, appreciation, and gratitude. With each breath in, imagine receiving that love, appreciation, and gratitude. This love should go from your heart to their heart. Take a few moments to just be in this state of love and appreciation with the animal, and feel this heart-to-heart connection with them.

Step 6 – Start with Simple Questions

As you continue to feel this loving connection between the two of you, start with simple, fun, chatty questions, such as "What is your favorite treat?" or "What is your favorite activity?" You are looking for small details you can verify with the owner so that you can be sure that you have a real connection.

Allow the thoughts to wash over you. Don't try thinking or forcing them, just allow them to come to you. Relax and see what comes to mind. An answer to your question should feel easy and flowing. What you get may not make sense. It may be a vision, feeling, thought, or some other sensation. Simply accept whatever you get.

As you ask these simple questions and are allowing the thoughts to come, you are getting a sense of the animal's personality and strengthening the connection. Continue to allow. Although this connection may start out weak or confusing, the energy will become stronger. You are building the energy connection. You want to receive as much information and a sense of personality as you can. Then talk to the owner for verification. This verification is not only for the owner, but it is also for you to be sure you have established a connection. You want to verify that you are receiving accurate answers and not ones that you could have easily guessed.

I start my sessions by asking my client not to tell me anything up front. I am looking for those "little gems" to confirm the connection. This confirmation does not usually come in the form of a great revelation or a major event from their life. More often than not, it is actually the little personal details that end up proving the connection. It is relaying those personal moments that touch the owner and give something special and meaningful to a reading.

Simple questions to ask:

- ❧ What is your favorite food?
- ❧ What is your favorite treat?
- ❧ What is your favorite toy?
- ❧ What is your favorite place in the house?
- ❧ What is your favorite activity?
- ❧ Do you go for walks?
- ❧ Do you go anywhere with mom or dad?
- ❧ What does your bed look like?
- ❧ Do you have other animal friends in your home?
- ❧ Tell me something funny or silly about yourself.
- ❧ Tell me something funny or silly about your mom or dad.
- ❧ What makes you happy?
- ❧ Do you like to run, jump, roll, dig?
- ❧ Where do you like to be petted?
- ❧ Are you old, young, energetic, slow?

For example, when you ask the question, "What is your favorite treat?" you are asking telepathically by imagining the question in your mind. You may immediately get a vision, or perhaps a knowing or a smell. Maybe you will imagine a bag of treats being opened. If so, ask what they taste or smell like. You may even hear the bag being opened or the treats dropping into your bowl.

To the animal, a treat may not always mean food. Perhaps their treat is playing with their owner or running on the beach. Allow the thoughts to wash over you and visions to come into your imagination. As a scene appears, ask, "What do you feel? What do you smell?" Ask for more details of the scene silently and telepathically.

Step 7 - Listen with Imagination and Heart

Allow your imagination to flow, thoughts to drift into your head, and feelings to wash over you. As you ask each question, pause to receive an answer. Allow the answer to drift back to you as a thought, imaginary vision, feeling, or sense that comes over you. Do not strain or search for an answer. If you don't receive anything, simply relax and go back to concentrating on sharing that loving connection. Then repeat the question. Pay attention to your body. How do you feel? Do you have a sensation that doesn't feel quite like it is yours? Do you have a twinge or a twitch in an area of your body? Perhaps the animal has an issue in that area.

Try the question, "What is your favorite food?" Pay attention to your very first thought after you ask the question. It may be only a word, snippet, or feeling. Whatever it is, take note of it. If a thought or an image does not come into your mind, try imagining what their food bowl looks like. Then fill it with something out of your imagination. You will be surprised that what you have "made up" often turns out to be their favorite food. Perhaps as you make up a food and fill their bowl, you will get the feeling that it is not correct and the image may change. This is the animal redirecting your thoughts. If the owner is present, let them know what you are getting as they may be able to give you positive feedback immediately.

You may not need to actively ask about the animal's personality. The sense of what their personality is like may have already started coming to you as soon as you connected. If it didn't, ask yourself "Am I shy? Am I outgoing? Am I excited? Am I young or old?" Imagine you are in the body of the animal and tune in to what your body feels like. If you have a tail, what is your tail doing?

Where are you? Are you outside or inside? How do you feel about this place? Now ask the animal to take you on a tour of their home. Ask where they sleep. You may get a certain type of doggie bed or you may find yourself inside your owner's bed! Start as if you were coming through the front door. Have them show you the kitchen and then take you around their house to the different rooms. The animal will see things that are interesting to them rather than what you as a person may find interesting. They may tell you things like, "There is a large tree in the hall and I like to sniff the leaves. There are two kitty litter boxes in the bathroom, one for me and one for my brother." This is a sort of remote viewing of the household. You are inside the body of the animal going around their home.

As you do this, it may feel like it is your imagination, and that's ok. Don't be afraid to use your imagination. That is often how you will get into the communicating zone. Also tune into what you feel in your heart. It may feel like a knowing or an intuition. You will sense deeper if you follow what your heart tells you.

Step 8 – Ask More Important Questions

Now that you have asked several light questions, got a sense of their personality, and received verification, go on to questions about behavior, health, and other issues. This is the time to ask more important or sensitive questions. Ask the questions that are significant to their owner, such as, "Why are you tearing up the corner of the couch?" or "What is going on with your health?" As with the simple questions, allow the answers to flow back through your imagination, allowing thoughts, visions, and feelings. In later chapters I will cover issues such as health and behavior more comprehensively.

After you feel you have received the answers to your questions, give the animal a chance to bring up their own topics. Ask them what else they would like to talk about or if they have something they wish to tell their owner. They may very well have a message they wish to get across or are concerned about something.

Step 9 - End Your Session. Thank the Animal.

At the beginning of the session the connection may have seemed weak or the answers not clear. As the session continued, the connection should have strengthened, and you should have felt the answers coming more easily. As the session now comes to a close, you may feel the animal's energy getting weaker and the communication becoming more distant again.

As you end the session, thank the animal for communicating with you. If you have made any promises during the session, such as, "You will receive your favorite treat every time you use your litter box," make sure that the owner agrees to stick to this promise. It is also good to offer a special treat or reward for having communicated. Make sure the owner gives their animal a big thank you and perhaps a good petting or rub for their effort to communicate with you.

Step 10 - Disconnect Your Energy

Disconnect yourself psychically, protect again, and ground yourself. To do this, just imagine pulling your energy back into your body and actually feel your fingers and toes. Imagine your bubble of white light protection around you. Then think of tree roots of white light going down into Mother Earth and connecting you to the earth.

10 Steps to Connect
Find a Quiet Place and Allow for Plenty of Time

Step 1 – Protect Yourself Psychically

Step 2 – Get in the Communicating Zone

Step 3 – Call in Your Animal Guides

Step 4 – Connect to the Animal

Step 5 – Heart-to-Heart Connection

Step 6 – Start with Simple Questions

Step 7 – Listen with Imagination and Heart

Step 8 – Ask More Important Questions

Step 9 – End Your Session. Thank the Animal.

Step 10 – Disconnect Your Energy

CHAPTER 7

How It Works

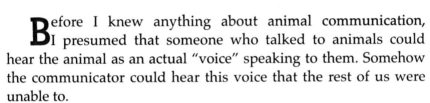

Before I knew anything about animal communication, I presumed that someone who talked to animals could hear the animal as an actual "voice" speaking to them. Somehow the communicator could hear this voice that the rest of us were unable to.

During my first attempt at animal communication, I expected to hear the animal "talk" to me. What I quickly learned is that you don't actually hear the voice of the animal nor do you see a vision appear in front of you. (At least I don't. Perhaps some people do!) Animal communication is much more subtle than that. In fact, it seems very much like your own thoughts coming to you. The animal's thoughts appear in the same way as your own thoughts, imagination, or memories do. The difference is that they come with emotions and images that feel like they don't belong to you.

I have come to believe that what really happens is that if we are open to this communication, an animal can send us their thoughts just as they would be formulated in their own mind. That is with all the background, personality, and emotions of their thought, along with the visual image they see in their mind. They are then able to place it into our thought pattern, and we receive this thought just like it was our own. But it is more than just a thought. It is actually a packet of information: a thought with a visual image, feeling, sense of being there, and even the backstory.

For example, if I asked you what you did last night, you would go back into your memory bank. Your eyes may actually look upwards to the left for a moment as you recall the memory. Perhaps you would find yourself recalling a romantic dinner you had with your loved one the night before. You might see the candlelit setting in your mind and remember the taste of the delicious meal. You'd recall the precious moments you shared, the feelings, and the emotions. This entire image would play as a video of the memory and the backstory, all as an instantaneous thought. It would even contain the information about whether this was a rare occasion, what you felt about your loved one, and whatever else happened that night.

You have accessed your memory bank and retrieved this thought as a scene, instantaneously and with emotion. Of course you can only verbally describe to me what you did and even then, you may only choose to share where you went and what you ate, leaving out the romantic description. Even if you wanted to, you could never share the real sensations of your experience with me. Your body language may add a bit to the description but nothing like the complete picture you saw in your memory along with all the feelings and emotions.

When an animal sends you a thought, they are able to place this thought directly into your thought process so that it feels very similar to retrieving a memory. They can leave out any information they want, but they can also send you the full emotional image.

Since the messages come to you through your own thought pattern, it is very easy to think it's all in your imagination or that you are making it up. This is often the point where many people give up, as they presume they've simply made it up. When you are connected through animal communication it does feel slightly different, but it is very subtle and can be easily misunderstood as your imagination. After a while, you get used to just knowing which are your own thoughts and which are the animal's. There are some distinct differences that let you know if you are tuned in and really receiving messages from the animal:

- ❧ The lightning speed at which the thought/answer comes to you.

❧ The emotions attached to the thought you receive are strong and perhaps unexpected.

❧ An unusual answer. Something unexpected that you don't think you would have made up on your own.

❧ Seeing through the eyes of the animal, literally from their perspective.

Lightning Speed

Once you have made a connection the communication comes back very fast, almost before you have completed your question. The animal's answer will pop into your mind nearly instantaneously. If you are trying to force an answer or trying to figure out the "correct" answer, you are trying too hard. If it is not coming quickly and easily, relax, go back through your steps, and try again. Sometimes you need to take a break to clear your mind and then try again later.

Your animal, or any animal for that matter, is already tuned into you and this type of communication. They are used to receiving your messages, whether you are meaning to send them or not. As you formulate your thoughts you are sending them out to the world, and the creatures around you are already picking up on them.

Your animal hears your question at your first thought. Before you finish formulating the question in your head, they have already heard it. Before you silently and consciously send the question to them, they know it. So while you are still formulating the right words for your question, they have long received it and are sending back their answer. If you are accepting and tuned in, you will receive their answer immediately and without effort.

This is why you are looking for the first thing that "pops into your head" even if you think it is wrong. This form of communication is more efficient than our verbal language and therefore much quicker. Sometimes the animal is so anxious and excited to talk to you that the thoughts will start popping into your head one after another before you even ask anything. Often the correct thought will come into your mind first and then you will dismiss it as you try to "think" of the answer. Just be open to accepting the first thing that comes to you, even if you don't think it fits what you are asking.

When you are asked a question about a specific event, you simply recall the event. You don't have to figure out which memory fits best. You just have the memory. It's instantaneous. It's easy and there is no effort involved. Animal communication is the same way. That is the reason for doing the preparation exercises: to get you to switch off your thinking brain and just allow this basic thought process to happen without interference. Relax and allow.

Sharing Emotions

A big indication that you are "hearing" the animal is if the intensity of an emotion that comes through is exceptionally strong or if an emotion doesn't feel like it should belong to you. Animals are wonderfully emotional creatures and their thoughts will come to you with their emotions attached. You may have an instantaneous feeling that you are talking with an excited young puppy or a reserved older cat and will get a general sense of their personality. As you begin to feel what their personality and physical body are like, you may become aware that you have an uncontrollable wagging tail and can barely hold in your excitement. Perhaps you may feel old and tired and can barely be bothered to talk. When they send you a message, you feel all their sensations with that message. This is because their feelings come along with the thought they send and you are actually experiencing their thoughts.

When we answer a question, we usually have some kind of emotional reaction to the subject we are talking about. Something that stirs us may elicit a strong emotion whereas a more mundane thought may just have a subtle emotion attached. However, that feeling is rarely translated to another person when we are communicating solely with words. If we do get a sense of a person's emotions, it is often conveyed by their body language, the look in their eyes, or by the vibe they give off, rather than strictly from the words that they use. Some experts say that around 75% of our communication is through body language and other types of non-verbal expressions and only around 25% is through the spoken word. In animal communication you are receiving the animal's thoughts as if they were your own, along with any feelings and sensations that accompany those thoughts. It is a much more comprehensive form of communication.

You may be surprised by the sensations that come across and they may not fit what your thinking brain expected. You may sense a smell that you don't recognize or it may be a smell that you dislike and, in this moment, you like it. The feelings that you receive toward something will be the feelings the animal would have toward it, not you. So when you sense the animal's thoughts, you may feel that you like a certain food that you know, in your own life, you don't like at all.

I was once invited over to a friend's house for a formal dinner celebration. At some point, I was introduced as being able to talk to animals and I soon found myself going around the table and being quite the party trick. I was enjoying stopping at each guest and trying to describe their animal and explaining its little quirks.

I stopped at one lady who had a young Golden Retriever. As usual, I started out by telepathically asking her pet a few light questions to get the communication going and to see if I could pick up any identifying tidbits. I asked my starter question, "What is your favorite food?" I was surprised to receive the instantaneous reply of "Yummmm, sweaty socks!" Along with the message, I received the full smell and emotion that went with this picture. I could actually smell these sweaty socks. I felt myself sitting in my doggie bed, chewing on these delicious morsels and drooling at the thought. The strange thing was that I was enjoying this smell and taste! I turned to the owner and sheepishly expressed what her dog had said, not knowing how she or the rest of the formal dinner party was going to take this. She laughed, "Oh, he's always in my laundry basket. He steals everything and I find my socks in his dog bed!" Clearly the emotions that came along with this thought were not my own!

While in the communication process, I have often found myself with feelings that I know are just not mine. I may find myself insanely fixated on a bacon treat bag being opened or feel like I am going to wag my butt right off while waiting by my food bowl for turkey scraps.

Most often of all, I feel so much love coming from the animal and almost always, they ask me to transmit this feeling to their human "parents." Their feelings are much deeper and more intense than those of most people. Sometimes the feelings are so overwhelming that my eyes well up with tears and I almost feel silly. I have to tell the owners that this is a good feeling and I am not sad. I am just feeling such intense unconditional love.

I have also felt great pain, grieving, suffering, fear, and everything in between. Sometimes they even have to dumb down their feelings to spare us the full extent of their pain. Animals have such depth of feeling and are connected to their emotions in a much more intensified state than we will ever be.

Unusual Answers

Expect the unexpected. In fact, the best answers are always something you never would have guessed. If you ask a dog, "What is your favorite treat?" and you get the answer bones, then it may be difficult to tell if you are really connected or if this was just an obvious answer because almost all dogs like bones. On the other hand, if they show you colored milk at the bottom of a cereal bowl and say "Dad's breakfast cereal" then you have something specific you can easily verify.

In one of my very first attempts, I was given a photo of a large German Shepherd. I instantly received the feeling of an older, refined gentleman who had since passed on. He was coming across as a real sweetheart and was sending his mother great love. "I had a good long life!" he said with loving gratitude. I identified some things about his personality, what he looked like, and how he had passed. His owner verified everything. She seemed comforted but remained composed. Perhaps I could have guessed these things.

Then I asked telepathically, "What was your favorite thing to do?" To which he replied, "Tell mom I loved the time she took me to see the geysers." He gave me the image of him and his mom walking through a wide-open grassy space on a beautiful day.

Behind him in the background was a huge spray of water coming out of the ground. I told the owner what I thought I had heard. "Oh my goodness!" his owner replied. "I took him to Yellowstone Park and we did see the geysers! It was a wonderful trip." I think I was even more thrilled than she. This was one of my first attempts at communication and I came away from it musing over and over, "Well, I couldn't possibly have made that up, could I...?"

Sometimes the answers are so far out of left field that it throws you for a loop and you're left wondering how to say it tactfully to the pet's owner. One dog, whose owner obviously cared enough to come and see me, wanted to get straight down to business. I asked the usual, "What's your favorite treat?" and the answer came back loud and clear, "That a**hole left me locked up in the house again!" Clearly there were other issues to be dealt with and the dog wanted to get past the small talk.

Animals are extremely smart. As I discuss in the following chapters, I actually believe we are communicating with their higher consciousness where they are able to access great pools of knowledge. Sometimes you may get an answer that surprises you because of the level of intelligence it denotes or the accuracy that comes with it. It may even be something that you've never heard of and you'll be surprised that the animal would even know such a thing. For instance, they can give you an obscure medical term or the complicated name of a drug they are taking. I've also heard many a profound statement from them. As much as I would like to take credit when that happens, I'm certain it didn't come from me!

Seeing Through Their Eyes

One of my very first attempts at communicating left me with no doubt that when we connect in this way, we actually see through the eyes of the animal and literally step into their bodies psychically.

I was given the picture of a beautiful black cat with stunning deep dark eyes. As I stared into those magical windows to the soul, I instantly found myself transformed into another time and space. In front of my eyes I saw two very large feet, each one almost bigger than myself. These feet were wearing pink fluffy slippers with a large fluffy ball dangling over the big toe. The slippers were at my eye level and they were going around and around in a circular motion. As I watched them intently, I could feel my head following back and forth, around and around. I was so excited by these moving slippers and most of all by the wobbling little fluff ball on the end. I could hardly contain myself. I was so mesmerized by the scene. As I took myself out of the zone for a second, I asked the owner, "Do you have a pair of pink slippers with a fluffy ball dangling on the end?"

She replied quizzically, "Yes, I do."

"And do you ride an exercise bike in the morning? Somewhere where your cat likes to sit and watch?" I continued.

"Oh, yes!" she said. "I have an exercise bike in my living room, and I try to ride every morning. My cat likes to sit next to me. Why? Does he like to watch me?" I could tell her emphatically that he loved to watch her. This was a great source of entertainment for him!

Seeing from the animal's point of view is another indication that you are connected and receiving messages. You may find yourself at the animal's eye level, looking at people's feet and ankles. You may find yourself inside a cage or curled up inside a hutch. Maybe you'll be surrounded by giant humans and be afraid of being stepped on, or you'll be looking down from a high tree branch, ready to pounce. This is a great indication that you are receiving messages from your animal and that you are allowing their thoughts to penetrate your thought processes.

Deciphering Images

At first you may dismiss the thoughts, images, and feelings that you are receiving as your own. You may say that you got nothing or that it didn't make sense and therefore couldn't have been right. It is a good idea to jot down all the bits of information that you get. They may not make sense to you at first or you may only get disjointed images. However, you will be surprised at how many facts you can verify! You'll discover that odd thoughts and feelings are connected to something that doesn't make sense to you, but it does to the owner.

There are many times that an image or a word comes through that means nothing to me, and sometimes it even seems so incidental that it is not worth mentioning. I have learned to not hold anything back and to say any odd images or words that I receive. What I think might be insignificant might be something profound to the owner.

I had a dog say he liked "ice cream cones in the park." It turned out there was a park with a children's area that had large ice cream cone tunnels. He loved to run through them. If I had just said he likes to eat ice cream it wouldn't have been as significant or made as much sense.

I read for a lady whose little dog had been killed by coyotes. He came through and talked about the incident. It turns out he was one of several little dogs in the family and he was killed trying to protect the others. The message came through with love for his owner and for the other dogs. He passed along a special message to his owner. He asked her to "take care of my two little girls." I presumed this was because two of the remaining dogs were female. It was more than that. He was actually the father of the two females, so they were literally his little girls. This is why I recommend passing on exactly what you are hearing or seeing and try not to change it to what you think would make more sense.

I asked a Jack Russell Terrier what he liked and he responded, "fresh clean water." I could have just said water, but I repeated it verbatim. The owner jumped for joy. "He had a health problem and we switched to bottled water. Now, everyday when I put down his water bowl, we have a little game where I shout 'fresh clean water' and that's his cue to come running."

Most of the time the images are not coming through as full descriptive videos. More often you have to keep asking questions until you have enough answers to put together the full picture. If you are not really sure what you have received, ask the question again in another way or ask if this is the correct answer and give them the opportunity to say "yes" and confirm it or to give you another image. The only way you can become confident enough to open your channel is to throw caution to the wind and just "have a go."

Many times you may just get an odd word that pops into your head. Just have faith in yourself to believe that you have received something from your animal and write it down or repeat it to the owner. Even if you feel silly in doing so, speak up. Don't be afraid to say anything out of fear of being "wrong." Remember there are no right or wrong answers. Sometimes it may mean nothing to the owner and that's ok. Maybe the meaning will become clearer to you or the owner later. It is more disappointing when the owner tells you something that was right on the tip of your tongue, but you hesitated to say it out of fear of being wrong.

How It Works on a Higher Level

I have come to believe that we are not actually connecting to the animal's thinking, conscious mind (physical mind). Rather we are communicating with the animal's higher self. This is why it doesn't matter if the animal is paying attention or not. I often have owners tell their pet, "Look at her. Sit still and pay attention," but really it doesn't matter. The dog can be running around the park, sniffing, and socializing. The cat can be asleep.

Their higher self that we are tapping into is a more knowledgeable self that knows the past, future, and in fact, has infinite knowledge. Meanwhile, your animal's conscious thinking mind may be preoccupied with sniffing a garbage can. It's as if there is a Universal Consciousness, a collective thinking mind that we are all a part of. Animals can easily draw from this Universal Consciousness that we have a harder time accessing.

Let's look at this Universal Consciousness for a moment. We are all energy beings, meaning we are all made up of energy. Our physical bodies are made of atoms, which consist almost entirely of space. The only reason we have a physical form is due to the vibration or energy of the atoms we are made up of. The space between us, in our atmosphere, and all through the galaxy is also made up of energy. So we all live together in a kind of vibratory energy field. Around our physical bodies we have a sort of halo or energy field, sometimes referred to as an aura.

When you look at it from this perspective, you can start to see that we are not really separate, but rather different forms of energy in the same energy field. Our thoughts and memories are not actually stored in our physical bodies, but rather our thoughts are energy, held in the universal energy field as part of the collective Universal Consciousness.

When you know the phone is going to ring before it does or you were just thinking about a person before they contacted you or you have a "feeling" something is going to happen, you are connecting into this Universal Consciousness. Does this mean you are psychic? Yes! We all are. Whenever we have intuitive thoughts and feelings, we are tapping into the Universal Consciousness. This is why when you practice animal communication, you develop your intuition, your connection to the Universal Consciousness, and you open up many other areas of psychic ability and spirit communication as well.

So when we connect telepathically, we are connecting to that part of the Universal Consciousness that is the higher self of the animal. If this concept is hard for you to intellectualize, don't worry. You don't need to know exactly how it works and it may be a millennium before we really even know. Just know that it does.

Is this concept anti-religious? No. In fact to me, Universal Consciousness *is* God. But God and religion is a personal matter and I am going to let you fit your own concept of God into this.

Animals Communicate in Unison

Animals are able to function as a team, as a collective. Just think about schools of fish. Have you ever noticed how hundreds of them swimming together will make a sudden turn and the entire school moves in perfect synchronization without missing a beat. There isn't one leader who makes the move and then the rest follow. It is an instantaneous event they do in unison. This is a perfect example of animals being connected telepathically. That is they are in sync and working from the collective consciousness.

There is a theory about collective consciousness thinking called the "hundredth monkey." This theory stems from research done by a group of scientists on the Japanese island of Koshima who tracked the learning abilities of monkeys. They described how the behavior of washing sweet potatoes started with the young monkeys and then spread throughout the colony. This understanding was passed from one monkey to another and continued to spread. Once a large enough group of monkeys understood the concept (supposedly around the one hundredth monkey), a sort of critical mass or threshold was reached, and suddenly monkeys on neighboring islands even had this new skill.

These new monkeys had no contact with the monkeys on Koshima and were even separated by the ocean. So how did this knowledge spread? One theory is that the monkeys were communicating telepathically or learning through the collective consciousness. So even though the monkeys were not in contact physically, they were still able to learn from their peers. I believe this is an example of a natural form animal communication that enables animals to communicate among themselves and through the collective consciousness.

Animals are able to place a "packet" of information into our mind. We receive this as a thought, just like it was our own. However, it is more than a thought. It is actually a packet of information: a thought with a visual image, feeling, sense of being there, and even a backstory.

CHAPTER 8

Personalities

There are quite a variety of personalities in the animal kingdom, just like there are among people. When you connect through animal communication, you will be surprised at just how much personality these little critters have.

Paco

I was doing mini-readings at a metaphysical shop in Los Angeles when a little Chihuahua named Paco came to see me (with his owner in tow, of course!). Instantly I perceived that he had a very macho personality and an adorable Mexican accent. (The accent could have been my imagination, having seen too many movies or fast food commercials, but it fit his personality perfectly.) He was wearing a multicolored doggie jacket and told me, "I'm waiting for the tuxedo, though. It's much more manly!" The owner confirmed that she makes outfits for him, and she was indeed in the process of making one in the design of a tuxedo.

He went on to talk about the Chihuahua girlfriend he was hoping for and that they'd been searching for just the right one. The owner confirmed this and talked about her search for a female Chihuahua. Macho man could barely contain his excitement. His imagination sent me a vision of girl Chihuahuas all lined up waiting for him. In his imagination, he went down the line and eyed each one. He was like a kid in a candy store. Each one was gorgeous in his eyes (and my thoughts) and then I stopped at one particular lady. "That's the one. That's the one!" he screamed excitedly. "The white one."

It turns out his owners had actually been to see a white female Chihuahua whom they were considering getting. However, they had also recently shown him the movie "Beverly Hills Chihuahua," so I wasn't sure if he was dreaming of the dog in the movie instead. But I'll tell you this; this dog was hot to trot! Then I paused for a second and did a double take. "Um...aren't you neutered?" I asked him. To which he responded with slight embarrassment, "Aw, we don't want to talk about that!"

Gender

Most of the animals I have encountered seem to place very little emphasis on gender. They seem to make friends just as easily with an animal of the same sex as they do with one of the opposite. Most of the time I find that they don't even consider what sex they are. I believe the owners are the ones who put the emphasis on whether they are a "boy" or a "girl" and treat them accordingly. Of course, Paco the Chihuahua was an exception!

Mimicking Their Owner

Sometimes an owner will tell me that their cat is mean and will take a swipe at them or bite them for no apparent reason. They may tell me that their dog is continuously anxious and fussy about everything, whining if they aren't being held. I'm reluctant to say it, but animals pick up their owner's energy and after being together a long time, often take on certain characteristics of their owner. So if your cat is grouchy and lashes out, look at yourself. Do you have a short fuse? Do you wish you could lash out sometimes? Do you get road rage?

For the fussy dog owner, are you too obsessive about details? Do you overstress and worry about things? I'm not saying this is bad as there are positive aspects of these qualities. However, if you want your cat to be sweeter or your dog to be calmer, let them know that you get it, and you will pay more attention to these traits in yourself.

The opposite is true as well. Someone who is laid back and mellow is likely to have a similar pet. The sweet angelic little critter is taking the lead from their owner, as well. It is like when owners and pets sometimes even grow to resemble each other. When you are on the same vibration and sharing energy fields, you attract and mimic one another.

Their Voice

You may get the feeling that your animal has a deep, slow voice or a high-pitched, excited voice. They may even have an accent. However, even the tone of their voice is translated to you as a feeling, rather than an actual voice you hear with your ears. What you perceive as the inflection of their voice is actually your mind interpreting the energy of their personality and converting it into a voice. Their personality assigns the tone and how it would come across to you if it were spoken.

If you are picking up on something specific in their tone, perhaps a Texan accent, you will usually find that there is some relevance to it. Perhaps the dog lived on a ranch in Texas and the owners moved to California. In that case, the dog wanted to bring across the wonderful memories of the ranch and sending the image of him speaking with a Texan accent was his way of expressing that his former home was in Texas.

Looks Can Be Deceiving

It is easier to start with a photograph of the animal subject instead of a live animal as this ensures that you are not being influenced by the animal's actions or body language. There may be obvious personality traits that you can see just by being around them, and you want to make sure that you can pick up on these vibes without actually having the animal in the room. Also, sometimes their appearance may contradict how they really feel. An animal may look old and tired, yet their personality comes through as perky and cheerful.

Bugsy

I met Bugsy in person. He was an old dog, probably around fifteen. He was lying by the fire and barely looked up as I came in. His fur was mostly grey around the face and his coat was very dull and patchy. His mom, Janet, had brought me in to see if it was time for Bugsy to leave this world. As soon as I saw him, I knew the news was going to be sad, as he wasn't long for this world. I sat beside him, and he looked at me out of one eye as if that was all he could muster.

I tuned in and began a conversation. He was surprisingly chatty. Then I asked him about his health and his time here. "I'm fine," he said indignantly. "Can't an old guy take a rest in front of the fire without someone thinking he's dying? I'd feel silly chasing a ball with the youngsters these days, but it doesn't mean I'm on my last legs." He assured me he had no major health issues and promised me that if it made Janet feel better, she could throw him a ball once in a while. The last I heard, Bugsy was still hanging in there.

Choosing an Animal

When choosing a new pet, tune in and get to know them on a deeper level. Find out about their personality and if you are compatible. This can help you to make the best decision for both of you. For example, if you tend to be a worrier and stress a lot, you may be better off with an animal who is calm and can help you to be more relaxed. If you choose an animal who wants to play and is rambunctious, make sure you have enough time and energy to play with them.

If you currently have other animals, include them in your decision-making process. Make sure your new addition is right for the whole family and that all of their personalities will fit well together. Not that their personalities need to be the same, but rather that they each have their own role in the family and are compatible, even if they are very different.

Pets and Their Jobs

Animals have different personalities and just like people, they like to fit into their household and get along with everyone. Animals also like to feel useful and have their own job. This is especially important when there is more than one animal in the household. Discord can develop in the group when one animal feels like another animal is trying to do *their* job.

What types of jobs relate to the animals in your household? See what their personality is and what they do best. Here are some examples:

- ❧ Meeter and greeter
- ❧ Protector
- ❧ Healer
- ❧ To bring fun
- ❧ To calm their owner
- ❧ To exercise their owner
- ❧ To teach love
- ❧ To help your creativity flow more easily
- ❧ To help you open up more psychically
- ❧ To care for the other animals in the household

When you have assigned a job to your animal, make sure you praise them for it. Tell them things like, "I really appreciate how much fun you bring into my life when we play. Thank you for welcoming my friends. You are such a good greeter."

Reggie

Laura called me about her cat, Reggie. Reggie was an older cat, maybe ten years old, but with lots of life still in him. He had always been a very reliable guy and never a problem. However, he had recently started wandering off and spending multiple nights out before returning home. This behavior was very unlike him.

This time Reggie had been gone for over a week, and Laura was getting really worried. I tuned in to find out if Reggie was ok and found him fairly close to home. He seemed a little surprised that he had even been missed. He didn't think he'd been gone that long and, besides, why did it matter? Reggie seemed fine, but why wasn't he returning? I did notice that he sounded a little depressed, and Laura asking about him seemed to cheer him up.

I asked him why he left. He explained that he had fulfilled his role and now another man had come into Laura's life. It was time to re-home himself into a place where he could be more useful. He was now helping out an older gentleman from time to time. Apparently one of Laura's neighbors was feeding Reggie, talking to him, and now he was hanging out there most of the time.

Reggie explained that he had been Laura's right hand for a long time. He would keep Laura company, make her laugh, play with her, but more than anything he was there to give her the love she needed. Reggie told me that recently Laura had been given a pair of kittens, two little boys who had lots of energy and were great playmates for her. "Did he feel they had taken over his role and that's why he felt he wasn't needed anymore?"

"No," he replied. "Mom found a really nice guy, the love of her life. He's a great guy and it's what she's always wanted. Now she's very content and gets all the love she needs."

When I asked Laura, she confirmed that she had a wonderful new man in her life. He had just moved in and they were planning to get married. But Laura loved Reggie very much and wanted me to let him know how much she wanted him back. Reggie was happily surprised. He loved Laura, too, but just felt that he wasn't needed anymore. I managed to convince him that the kittens were just for playtime and that Laura's new guy was very special, but no one could take Reggie's place. Laura told Reggie that he had a very important role in her life. Sure enough, Reggie returned home the very next morning. Laura made a big fuss over him and even put his picture on her nightstand. The frame read "Lover Boy."

Originally Reggie had been a multitasker. As the only man in Laura's life, he took on the role of entertainer, protector, and love provider. His role was redefined for him to concentrate on just the love part. Laura's new guy loved him as well.

Reggie has occasionally taken off again but never for more that one night. Laura is not sure, but she thinks he still goes visiting the old man a few blocks away. Perhaps Reggie has a double role now.

CHAPTER 9

What's in a Name?

Names are hard to get. Usually when they come, they just pop into your head. It's a little bit like trying to remember the name of a teacher from elementary school. You rack your brain and then hours later, when you least expect it, the name just pops into your head. This is what it feels like when an animal communicates its name.

Getting the name exactly right is also difficult. You just have to trust and say the first thing that comes to mind. Straining to guess the name usually never works. Just allow and see what comes easily.

Sometimes you pick up on the energy of the name, getting its quality, but not it exactly. For example, you may only get the first initial correct. That is you intuit that it is a "B" name, but say Buster instead of Brandy. You may get a sound that could have been slightly misunderstood, such as Sandy instead of Randy. Perhaps you correctly intuit that it is a flower name, but get Buttercup when the name is Daisy. Sometimes you may think you are completely wrong, such as when you get Joe instead of Max or Crystal when her name is really Princess. But actually you are on the right track because the names have a similar energy. Joe and Max are short, common, three-letter male names. Crystal and Princess both give you the feeling of pretty, cute, and pampered. Can you see how these have similar energy? Keep saying the first thing that pops into your head and eventually you'll get it.

You may also get a visual image that represents the name. For example, if you see an image of a striped t-shirt and the animal's name is Stripes. Some people who attend my workshops actually see a ticker tape or television screen with the name written on it.

Muffin

I was doing a reading for a woman who lost her cat and tuned in to start tracking the cat's location. When I asked some simple questions for identification, a name popped in my head. "Is the cat's name Muffin?" I asked. She said no. A little thrown I said, "Is it Muppet or Muffler or something similar? "No," she told me again. I continued with the tracking and talked to her cat who was alive and well. She promised that she would come home. However, I kept getting the name "Muffin" so I checked one last time with the owner. Her response was still a definite, "No." The next day the woman called me ecstatic. "You'll never guess. My cat came back! She's here safe and sound. My Cupcake came back!" Yes, her name was Cupcake!

As you can see, our translation of the energy of a name does not always sound similar to the actual name. I didn't actually see an image of a muffin. The name popped into my head as a word. What had happened was the cat relayed a packet of information to me that had the essence of "Cupcake" and I interpreted it as "Muffin." I was influenced by how my own mind recognized and interpreted this packet. This shows how we shouldn't be discouraged if we are getting something that isn't immediately recognized by either the owner or ourselves. Sometimes the owner may not even catch something that you'd think would be easily recognizable to them. Just stick to your steps and stay confident.

Pepe

When I was doing sample readings at one of my live events, I was drawn to one particular guy in the audience. I could feel his little dog who had passed coming through. He was still distraught over his little one's passing. A name popped in right away. "Was his name Pepe?" I asked. "No," he replied. "His name was Gordon." (Or something completely different is what I thought….) Then he added, "but I used to call him Pepe"–A-ha!

Whatever you call your animal is going to be what they think their name is. So if you call them "little one" or "my darling" that is what they think their name is. Even if they know it is a nickname, they will use it to identify themselves because that is what you call them most often.

There's an old joke that goes something like this:

- ❧ Two dogs meet in the dog park, a white one and a brown one.
- ❧ "What's your name?" asks the brown one to the white one.
- ❧ "Bad Dog Get Down," answers the white one.
- ❧ "Nice to meet you. I'm No Stop It," replies the brown one.

Be Thoughtful How You Name Your Animal

Be careful what you name your animal. Animals will often grow to become like their name as they think this will please their owner. They understand the energy of the name. It always astounds me when someone names their dog Killer or Striker and they wonder why they turn out to be vicious.

Don't Use Their Name in Punishment

If your dog runs to the door barking and you try to stop them, don't yell their name. If Molly is barking, don't shout, "Molly!!!" This teaches them that you are angry or disappointed with them whenever you call their name. Instead, use their name often in a very positive, encouraging way. "Molly, you did a really good job at staying relaxed when the mailman came. Molly, you're a wonderful dog."

Ask for the animal's name and
then allow the thoughts to come back.

Don't try to force it or strain to guess a name.

If a name pops into your head, just say it.

Don't worry if you don't get a name. Try not to place too
much emphasis on getting a name in a session.

CHAPTER 10

Pets in Spirit

Communicating with an animal who is living feels very similar to communicating with one who has passed away and is in spirit. They both communicate in the same way and you cannot always tell if the animal you are reading is alive or has passed on unless you ask them directly.

Talking with an Animal in Spirit

You connect with an animal in spirit in exactly the same way as you do with an animal who is alive. Start by asking them simple questions. They are going to tell you the things they liked when they were alive. I'm sure these are the things they are continuing to do on the other side.

When you ask about health, they are going to tell you the ailments that they had while they were living. They no longer have these ailments. This is just so you can identify who they are and verify your connection. They may also tell you how they passed.

What If You Are Uncertain

Sometimes an owner is not sure if the animal has passed, such as if the animal is missing or has been given away. If you are having a difficult time figuring out if they are alive or have passed, you can ask them. Usually they tell you straight out or you will get a sense by their answer. For example, if you ask an animal with serious health issues how they are feeling and they say how wonderful they feel, this is likely a sign that they have passed already.

Occasionally a pet will not want to tell you that they have passed because they wish to spare mom and dad's feelings or there may be some other reason they feel it is better for them not to know. Whatever the message is, just pass on what you feel. It is ok to say that you are not getting a clear answer.

Animals Connect with the Other Side

Animals do not have the same fear of death that we do. Passing over to the other side is a normal transition for them (as is reincarnation). Animals can easily tap into the spirit realm and sense animals in spirit that are around them. Have you ever seen an animal acting like it is playing with another animal, but nobody is there? Perhaps you've seen your pet appear as if they are looking at someone, but they are staring into thin air. It may be that there is an animal in spirit around them who we cannot see ourselves. They may even be playing with this animal in spirit.

I have often been told by an animal in spirit that they want their mom or dad to adopt another pet. The person may say, "I could never do that. It would be like replacing them and I couldn't bear it." However, the dog in spirit may be saying, "We used to go on walks down to the stream and play fetch with sticks. Now my owner doesn't go anymore. If they get another dog, I can still come on the walks!"

Sometimes our animals are even able to travel outside of their bodies. Cats, for instance, have told me they leave their bodies at times and go to other realms, planes, and dimensions, including the spirit world. Meanwhile you just think they're sleeping. That may be where they were when they woke up with a jolt and fell off the TV!

Animals Stay with Us in Spirit

I have seen many examples of pets who after they pass, stay around their mom or dad. In fact, this seems to almost always be the case. When you have a strong bond with an animal, they continue that bond on the other side. You may still sense them sitting in their favorite chair or lying at the foot of your bed. Some even say they have more freedom now to be around mom or dad and can more easily help them from the other side.

When they are ready, your pets will often reincarnate and come back into your life. This is why we often have a familiarity with our animals, like we've known them before. You probably have when you were younger and perhaps even in a past life.

Animals and Our Relatives in Spirit

Often an animal who has passed will be with other family members who have passed as well. Letting you know whom they are with is another way for them to show you that they have passed. For example, they may say, "I am with the aunt who lived by the beach." If that relative has passed, then it is a sign that the animal is in spirit, too.

Sometimes your animals are needed to take care of other loved ones in spirit. During a reading I might get that your bird is now with your dad in spirit. Dad still likes to share his apples with her. If a beloved pet passes shortly after their owner has passed, you can bet they are still together in spirit.

Communicating with Your Own Pet in Spirit

I know that emotionally it can be very difficult to try to talk to your pet in spirit, but trust that your beloved pet is around you. Follow the steps in the same way as if your animal were alive. At first it may be difficult because you'll question whether you are really connecting with them or if it is your own wishful thinking. I can tell you this for sure, they are listening, they are around you, and they do hear you. Usually the best way to convince yourself that you can connect is to get more experience with other people's animals first. This builds confidence in your skills so you can better believe it when it comes to your own pets.

You can ask your pet in spirit a question or ask them specifically for a sign that they are there. Pay attention the next few days. You may see an image, object, or hear a comment that is your sign and the confirmation that you were asking for.

Our own animals in spirit often come to us in dreams. In the dream state we can more easily accept spiritual communication. If you have a dream about your pet in spirit (or even alive for that matter) and it seems particularly vivid, it was probably a visit from them. I have my own personal story to share on this:

My Dog Bob

I had my first animal communication experience many years before I became a medium and had any knowledge of the subject or my abilities. My first communication was with my dog Bob who had managed to talk to me in a dream.

Bob, like most of my menagerie of animals, showed up as a stray. He came to us shortly before we moved to the ranch. Somehow he ended up on our front porch and literally knocked on the door. My young daughter rushed ahead of me to answer the door and was licked to pieces. This cute little rascal was a lab mix who had one ear standing straight up and the other ear bent down. After having him for a month and falling in love, one of our neighbors recognized him from the "found dog" flyers we had put up. The day they showed up to take him we were heartbroken.

Luckily the couple came back the next day and said, "We really think he'll have a great life with you and we would like you to have him." This is how Bob became our trusted ranch dog. At this point in my story, Bob had already had a long full life with us. He was, in fact, a tough old man who was getting a little arthritic and now had a three-beat limp in his stride. This, of course, may have been more the result of his many battles than of old age. Bob had been through the wringer, literally.

The night before the 1994 Northridge earthquake in Los Angeles the wild animals may have anticipated that something terrible was about to happen. Their behavior was very much out of the ordinary. This was the night that Bob was attacked by a mountain lion. We knew they lived in the area, but to come so close to the house was quite unusual. Amazingly, after a three-hour surgery, being in the middle of an earthquake zone, then months of recovery, he survived the attack. Although the vet regrettably told us that, unfortunately, the one ear would probably never recover and will stay permanently bent. We laughed. This had always been his cute distinguishing factor.

Believe it or not, after his long months of recovery and on his very first night back out, he was attacked again by another mountain lion. Normally they are not known for attacking big dogs. However, an unfortunate distinguishing feature of Bob's was a little bobtail. On its own this would have been innocent enough, but he also had a white streak on the tan fur that made it look just like a deer's tail. Perhaps from behind, the mountain lion thought he looked like easy prey. From then on, nighttime pursuits were banned. Bob was given a curfew. He could be the brave ranch hand by day, but was the cute housedog by night.

By now his many battle injuries were clearly affecting this old dog, but we figured he still had a few more good years in him. It was then that I had a dream. Now I don't usually dream very often or at least I don't remember my dreams. This dream was really upsetting. I dreamt that as I was driving and about to turn up the road home, I saw Bob lying there beside the road.

"What are you doing here?" I asked.

"Well," replied Bob, "it's my time and I've come here to pass away quietly."

I was shocked and distraught, "What do you mean?"

Bob continued trying to let me down as gently as possible. "Mom, it really is my time. I'm old and tired. My body is done and it's my time to go. I know that if I'm at home, you and your mom will keep fixing me up. But this time, I don't want fixing. It's really, really, my time to go."

I was extremely sad, but somehow in my dream I took this news better than I would have in real life. "At least come back to the ranch so that you can be with the other dogs, and you can be buried there."

I woke up in tears, very disturbed. Oh, what a horrible dream! I was intensely upset about it. I ran to see Bob who looked perfectly fine. I was relieved. It was only a dream. However, it continued to bother me throughout the day. I kept checking in on Bob, and he looked quite happy and healthy. I talked to my friends and relayed my dream. They comforted me by saying things like, "You know dreams can mean the opposite. So it probably means he is going to live a long life."

A few days went by and we had a friend staying with us at the ranch. He had a young pit bull. He was a friendly sort but we thought it best that he was tied up if his dad was out.

We'd all gone out for the afternoon and tied up or not, something had taken place. Bob had obviously taken it upon himself to show his authority over this fellow and the young dog had gotten the better of him. We found Bob in a little gully close by, covered in deep brush. Bob's face was swollen, and his cheek was ripped and bleeding.

We immediately took him to the emergency vet. "Well, it looks pretty bad because of all the blood in his mouth, but really it's just a few cuts. I'm sure he's going to be okay," the vet assured us. However, he agreed to keep him overnight for observation.

The next day I took him home, but he was still not any better. In fact, now his face had completely swelled up like cartoon dog. I called the vet and told him that it looked like swelling from a snakebite, but I was assured it was just his age and the location of the bleeding. "He'll be ok," the vet insisted. That night I sat with him on the bathroom floor, Bob's face resting on a pile of ice. His face was still burning hot, and he lapped water from my hands.

Of course, now I'm thinking about the dream I had. "Well, maybe it was a dream representing the opposite and it was to reassure me that he'll be ok." I try to convince myself of this, but it doesn't work. I'm worried about him; I'm very worried about him. By morning he was not any better, so I took him back to the vet for another day of observation. The vet was reassuring once again, "Well, I don't see any major damage. It's just taking time. We'll keep him overnight again."

The next morning, I got a phone call. "I'm sorry. Your dog passed away last night." I stammered in disbelief, "How could this have happened?" I thought to myself, "The vet told me he'd be ok. He told me it wasn't that bad. Why would he tell me this if it hadn't been true?" My heart sank. The pain ripped me apart. I had lost a very good friend.

Yet through all this devastation, there was a little glimmer of gratitude. Gratitude that he had been able to let me know beforehand and that he had tried to prepare me. I was thankful that I knew this was what he really wanted. Thankful that I didn't have to now question if this had been the right time.

A few days later, a massive rattlesnake was spotted slithering out of the brush-covered gully exactly where Bob had been found. Had Bob received two separate injuries that day? If only I had seen this venomous creature, I would have insisted on treatment for Bob. But if he had received a second injury, a fatal snakebite, I knew that it had been Bob's choice that we didn't know.

Bob's girlfriend, Nala, our old blonde lab knew. She moped around like she had lost her husband. They had loved each other so much and spent most afternoons lying side by side grooming each other. Now she was lost.

About a week went by and I had another dream about Bob. In this dream, Bob came to me and said, "Don't be mad at the other dog. It's not his fault. It was my time. I wanted to go. This is how I wanted to go. I didn't want to suffer. I love you." Then he turned to leave and said, "I'll be back in a while. I will only come for a short time just to let you know I'm okay, but I will come back." I woke up and pondered my odd but comforting dream.

Around six to nine months later I woke up one morning to the sound of incessant barking. Nala was barking and barking down by the front entrance to our property. My mom went to investigate and received a complete fright. There was this dog sitting by the gate that was the absolute spitting image of Bob. He had one ear up, one ear down, and was the same color, breed, the same everything. He looked exactly like Bob.

Nala was over by this stray dog who just wandered onto the property. She was licking him, loving him, and was glued to his side. Nala obviously thought this was Bob, too. As you may know, dogs recognize by their sense of smell, not by sight. So Nala believed this was Bob, but not because of the physical characteristics that we recognized. Nala's reaction was confirmation enough for us. She was all over him and happy as a lark. She would not leave this dog's sight.

My mom said to me, "You know this is amazing. Who is this dog?" He was a younger dog, maybe six to nine months old, which was the same amount of time Bob had been gone. That combined with his physical similarities and Nala's reaction, we were all pretty freaked out.

Although this dog looked just like Bob, he was shy. At first he was too scared to come inside the house and would stay just outside. Nala also refused to come in the house. Nothing could get her to leave the side of this dog she believed was Bob. They sat together outside for a few days until finally, we managed to coax him inside.

We adopted him. It was official. This was Bob II. He looked and acted just like Bob. I remembered my dream and what Bob had told me. It had been about six months or so since his passing and here is a dog of around the same age.

We'd only had him maybe two or three weeks and were about to take him to the vet for his shots and to be neutered when all of sudden he just disappeared. We came back one day and he simply wasn't there. Had he heard me talking about having him neutered?!

We searched and put up flyers, but he was gone just like Bob had said in the dream. "I'm going to come back for a while, but I'm not going to stay. I just want to let you know I'm okay." Ever since that day, Nala has been herself again. She's been happy. I truly believe that it had been Bob.

Sometime after that, Bob popped in again one more time. My daughter had been trying to print out her homework on her computer, and when she hit the print button, out came a photograph of Bob. It looked a little eerie as this photo of Bob lying on the porch was superimposed over another image, but it was clearly Bob. My daughter came running upstairs in total disbelief. She said, "I don't have this photo on my computer. I actually don't have any photos of Bob on my computer. I looked and looked, but there's nothing. I just hit print, and this is what came out." I smiled at his photo and said, "Thank you, Bob."

I think animals and people do come through to us in dreams, especially if they can't get through to us in other ways because we are simply not listening or unaware. I was not the ideal subject because I don't usually remember my dreams, but Bob was determined to get through. I have him to thank for my first real animal communication.

Animals stay around us after they have passed.

Animals are more comfortable with
this transition than we are.

Animals in spirit are often with
our own passed over relatives.

Animals can easily communicate
with the spirit world.

Animals play with other animals in spirit.

Our animals in spirit are listening to us.

CHAPTER 11

Health Issues

If your pet has a health issue, animal communication can help give you insight into what is going on. Your pet may even be able to solve a mysterious health problem that you have been unable to figure out. Animals are very in tune with their body. They usually know what is ailing them and sometimes they know what will make them feel better or even cure them. I find that they may be quite aware of what medicines they are being given, if they agree with their treatment, and even have opinions about whether they like their vet.

What may surprise you is that many of their health issues are tied into the health or emotional issues of their owner. Communicating with your pet may not only help their health, but your own as well.

Animals are very sensitive to energy. They know when their energy is off-balance and how to correct it. They even remove negative energy from their owners. Being such sensitive creatures, they respond well to energy healing.

How to Ask About Health Issues

You are going to connect with the animal in the same way that we have already learned. The animal may be sensitive about a health issue, so start by gently chitchatting about fun activities or other simple questions. You want to make sure that the animal feels relaxed and trusts you. It is important to develop a rapport and start a dialog before asking more intimate health questions. Also, have the owner confirm this feedback to verify your connection so you can be confident in your answers before you ask more detailed questions. Then you can move on to more in-depth health questions.

1. Follow the steps to connect.

2. If this is not your own pet, start with easy questions that you can confirm with the owner to verify the connection.

3. Continue with light conversational questions (e.g., favorite activity) to be sure the animal is comfortable and at ease.

4. Ask the animal what they would like to share about their health.

5. If the animal has a health issue, ask them to describe the problem and what they feel.

6. Notice any feelings in your own body (e.g., slight aches or tingling).

7. If it is not clear where the health issue is located, do a body scan (explained on page 92).

8. Use a pendulum to check for chakra blockages or to get yes/no answers. (See appendix A for more information.)

9. Once a health condition has been identified, ask what is being done (e.g., taking medicine, seeing the vet).

10. Ask the animal if this condition is something that is curable. Ask if it is their karma to get well or to pass away.

11. Is there anything causing this condition (e.g., environment, age, energy transfer)?

12. Are they mimicking someone else's health condition?

13. Are they hanging on and staying in their physical body for someone?

14. What would make them feel better? Would a dietary change be helpful? (Always check with your vet before implementing any changes.)

15. Do energy healing or send the intention for them to be healed.
16. Invoke their guardian angel and other animal spirits for healing assistance.

* Note – A health condition may be communicated from a passed over animal in order to help you verify their identity.

What Is Causing Their Issue?

Ask your animal what is causing their issue, particularly if it is something new. If you have ruled out them mimicking the injury of an owner or someone they are close to, or having trouble transmuting negative energy from these people, then ask them about their environment. Have they moved? Is their owner using a new cleaning product? Has their food changed? Was there an accident or an incident?

Their issue may have more than one cause. For example, the animal may be having an allergic reaction to a chemical that was sprayed, but the owner may also have breathing problems that he or she has not taken care of. In other words, the owner's breathing problems are really the trigger and, in order to show this, the animal develops an allergic reaction. If there were no lesson to be shared, then the animal probably wouldn't have been allergic to the chemical in the first place.

The Diagnosis

When you have discovered a health issue, ask the animal if it can be healed and what they would like you to do to help them. Sometimes they actually know the proper medical term for a drug or a treatment they need or are currently receiving. Other times they might say, "I get a pink pill in the morning before I eat" or "the pill makes my tummy feel bad, but I know I need it."

They may also give you an odd answer for what they need, such as broccoli or oranges. Of course you should never take what they say as gospel. Check with your veterinarian before giving them anything. Animal communication is not an exact science and you do not want to be wrong on something like this.

Use your common sense. Listen to what your animal says, but remember animal communication is not 100% accurate. You should never go against your vet's advice because of what you think the animal has communicated. You may have misinterpreted what they said. You can ask your animal if they like and trust your vet or if there is another vet they prefer. I've been told, "I like the lady vet better because she is gentle and uses homeopathy. The guy I usually go to is not as patient."

If you believe your animal is saying something that goes against your vet's advice, you should talk to the vet, do your own research, and perhaps seek a second opinion. Animal communication may be used in conjunction with medical care (diagnosis and treatment), but should never to be used as an alternative.

Sampson

Sampson was a little guy with a big personality. He was getting older and had some pretty serious kidney issues. He was on medication and needed regular visits to the vet. When I asked him what would help his health he replied, "That rice pudding mom used to make with the cream on top." His mom responded in surprise, "But the vet said you can't have that!" Then Samson copped to it, "Aw shucks! But it was worth a try!"

Sense Through Your Own Body

We are energy-sensitive beings. Your animal can show you what areas to address by giving you a slight tingling or uncomfortable feeling in the same area on your own body. You are using your clairsentient sense to feel what they are feeling, and you are also receiving messages from the animal who transmits this message through a "feeling" they give you. This feeling doesn't hurt and it goes away as soon as you acknowledge it.

Even before asking a question you may, for example, feel your ear twitching or your elbow aching. As soon as you have connected with the animal, you may instantly get a feeling in your body that gets your attention. Or as you ask a question such as, "Tell me about your health," a feeling may just appear in your body. As you imagine yourself inside the animal's body, tune into what your own body feels like. Even if the ache seems to actually be a little tweak that feels like yours, it's probably not. I once asked a dog with worms if he had any health issues. I can tell you this; I was very relieved after I had passed on that message and my bottom stopped itching!

Does the Owner's Ailment Match?

Because we become in tune with our pets and our energy is so closely intertwined with theirs, they can mimic our own health problems. They are expressing the energy that we are exuding. For example, if a dog has a right back leg that hurts, I ask if the family member to whom the dog is closest has a right leg issue as well. More often than not they do. A pain in the right leg can also be associated with not moving forward on an emotional issue. Perhaps this person has a relationship they need to move on from and is scared to do so. Sometimes the animal wants to make their owner aware of an issue or there is negative energy that has built up. Often as soon as the person acknowledges what is going on and promises to address the health or emotional issue, the animal is instantly better.

So, one of the first questions I ask when an animal has a health issue is what is going on health-wise with the owner or the person closest to this animal. Many times you'll find that the person has an issue in their life as well.

Sandy & Rick

Bunny came to me about her dog Sandy who had an arthritic right hip. The dog wasn't that old but would often run with a skip or a limp. Some days were worse than others. I asked Bunny if she had a bad hip. She didn't but her husband Rick, who was closest to Sandy, had severe problems with his right hip. Over the years, he'd had many surgeries but was still in pain. Some days felt better than others. He had physical therapy exercises that he was supposed to do but often skipped them.

I did a healing on Rick's right hip and he miraculously stood up straight for the first time in years. Bunny called the next day to report that even more miraculously, Sandy, whom I hadn't even worked on, was healthy and acting her young self again as well. Sandy had been showing dad that he needed to pay attention to his hip. She wanted dad to do his exercises so he could get better.

Unfortunately, Rick's hip problem slowly returned and after about a week, he had pain and weakness once again. Just as dad's health reverted, so did Sandy's and her limp retuned. I've worked on them both several times since. Each time I only needed to work on Rick for them both to feel better, and each time their symptoms later returned. Dad needs to work on his own health and emotional issues so that they can both be permanently healthy.

Animal Body Scan

If you don't immediately get a message, try doing a body scan. If the animal is present, hold your hands about two inches away from their body and use your hands to scan them. This is sometimes called Gestalt therapy or a Gestalt scan. Basically you are tuning in to see if you sense any changes in their energetic field. You may feel a tingling in your hands or changes in temperature over a specific area as you run your hands along their body. As you scan, ask the animal if there are any issues in the area where your hands are currently located.

Start by looking at their head and ask, "Are there any issues with your head?" Then ask specifically about their eyes and ears. Move down to their throat, heart, and then to the rest of the body, continuing to ask at each point. I like to do the following order (after the head): one front leg, then the other front leg, down the back, across the front (belly), to the back left leg and then the back right leg. Listen for messages. Sense the energy in your hands, and also note any feelings in your own body as previously discussed.

If you are using a photo for your session, that will work just as well. Look at each part of the body in the photo and imagine that you are scanning the animal.

Burt

Burt was a cheeky little mixed-breed dog. Mom met me at a psychic fair and asked me to check if everything was good healthwise. Burt didn't have any immediate things he could think of so I did a body scan. As I get to his right front paw, I felt an old injury that had been fixed with a splint years earlier. Mom confirmed this. Then as I ran my hand down his spine, it felt perfectly normal until I got to the base. There was a little ouchy feeling just under my tailbone. Burt told me, "Oh, yes. I went to the vet and had that fixed. It's all good now." Mom guessing the cause, explained to me, "We went to the vet and, you know, when they get those impacted anal glands and the vet puts his finger up there and squeezes it out...."

Burt looked mortified and shot her a look, "Aw, mom! Do you have to tell her everything!!!?"

Spaying and Neutering

Sadly there is an overpopulation of uncared for animals and it is tragic that so many end up homeless and in animal shelters. It is very important that you spay and neuter your animals. They understand and are quite happy to go through this. The females say the operation is not particularly pleasant, however most say it is better than dealing with being "in season." Almost all agree that it is necessary. Very rarely do they care about being a neutered animal. Occasionally I find one who misses being a mom, but they are usually quite satisfied to look after the other animals in the home. I had a dog, Penny, who fostered a little kitten I rescued. She treated that little kitten just like it was her own!

Cats Acting Tough

I often find that cats act tougher than they really are. You can talk to a cat with his leg hanging off, and he'll tell you that he's fine. "What, my leg? Oh no, that's nothing!" This is instinctive. In the wild a predator will go for those who are injured and therefore are easy prey. So cats are wired to act like everything is fine, even when it's not. They are also proud animals who prefer minimal fuss. When it's their time to pass over, they often prefer to just wander off somewhere quietly and die in peace.

When It's Time to Let Go

An animal knows when it is their time to go. You can tune in to your animal and ask them if their illness can be cured and do they want to continue living. Sometimes you will get the message that it's their time. They may say that their body is too old, they are too ill to save, or that they are suffering too much.

I don't think I've ever heard an animal say that they were put to sleep too soon. However, many of them will say that they hung on longer for mom or dad. Almost always when you get the sense it is their time, it usually is.

Animals don't have the same fear of death that most of us have. They are much closer to the spirit realm and understand that dying is simply passing from one form to another. They know they will continue to be around us in spirit and that they can come back again. In fact, I've found that cats sometimes even leave their physical bodies while they appear to be sleeping. The spiritual realms are not so far away for the animal kingdom.

Sometimes an animal will hang on for us until we have come to terms with their impending passing. They may try to help us understand the transition and sometimes they'll even wait until they find us a replacement. This is why another animal may happen to show up, needing to be rescued, a few days before or after our pet's passing. When this happens, it is not a coincidence. This is your pet making sure that their duties will be covered or that you will continue to have companionship after they leave.

Approach an animal with sensitivity
about a health issue.

What does your animal's health say about
your own health?

Check your home for changes in the
environment or causes of ailments.

Ask what foods or remedies would help them.
(Make sure they're telling the truth
and not fishing for a treat.)

Is your animal acting tough when
they are really in pain?

Be respectful when they choose to pass over.

Our animals remove and
transmute our negative energy.

Energy Healers

As I am sure you know, our pets bring us great health benefits. Just stroking and loving our pet is calming and reduces stress. In fact, therapy animals have become commonly used to help those who are ill, elderly, developmentally disabled, or dealing with other serious issues. It is medically proven that stroking our pets actually reduces our heart rate and calms anxiety. But really it's much more than this. Animals remove negative energy from around us, in our auras, and even from our physical bodies. They are able to remove this negative energy from us, process it, and release it. Because of this ability, some animals feel their specific purpose in life is that of a healer.

For example, when we come home from work stressed out and our dog comes to lie next to us or rests his head on our lap while we stroke him, he is actually absorbing our stress, processing the negative energy, and releasing it. I'm sure you've noticed how your worries and stress all seem just a little bit easier to manage after a few minutes of cuddling with your animal.

When you were sick, has your pet jumped into your lap? Have you ever had an injury and your dog or cat came to lie next to you or the injured area? An animal will often lie directly on or next to our body part that is injured. They know exactly where we need the healing.

Imagine that we have an energy aura around us that sometimes gets murky or dusty. Our animals can help to clear this aura. If they are healthy, they can take that energy and transmute it into positive energy very easily. However, when an animal gets older or receives too much of an overload, they will have a more difficult time processing it and can even get ill. It is not a very nice thought that we can sometimes contribute to our pet's health problems, especially since animals are totally selfless. However, they believe it is their purpose and are quite happy to help us to release our stresses. We can help them by doing our own part and asking our spirit guides to clear our energy and de-stress us before coming home to our pets. I'm also told that fresh clean spring water, fresh air, and being in nature helps our animals process this negative energy.

Winston

I had a client who asked me about his cat, Winston. Winston was a large, very old cat and his owner was concerned about his health. I felt that the overall issue had to do with the blood. I got the word "HIV." This was strange, I thought, but the owner confirmed he had a similar disease carried by cats. I also felt a lot of troubled energy.

It felt almost like a "homeless, drugs, street mentality" energy. I asked what this man did for a living that could give his cat this energy. He told me that he worked as a therapist for homeless drug addicts, many with HIV. I explained to him that before he comes home from work, he needs to clear off any of this energy. Before he walks in the house, he should take a moment to ask the spirits to remove any negative energy so his cat won't absorb it. "Oh no, it's more than that!" he said. It turns out these people come to his home office and Winston sits under the table during the sessions.

Just by understanding this energy exchange, the owner was able to better take care of his cat. By limiting Winston's time at therapy sessions, providing him with fresh clean water, and placing crystals in his space, I am happy to say his health is now greatly improved.

Healing Yourself to Heal Your Animal

When your animal is ill, also look at yourself, both physically and emotionally. What is going on in your body that your animal could be showing you? Sometimes our physical ailments have not yet shown up or our animal has manifested the illness instead of us.

For example, if we have a negative relationship that we are allowing to go on for a long period of time, it can create negative energy around our Sacral Chakra (the energy center about two inches below our naval that is associated with relationships). If we continue to allow this stressful relationship situation, it may eventually manifest in issues in the reproductive area. Alternatively, your animal may develop the physical issue instead. This is because they have removed the negative energy from you before it manifested physically in your body. So when you look to yourself, look at unhealthy emotions or possible negative situations.

My daughter is a vegetarian who doesn't like vegetables and essentially lives off pizza and the like. Of course as much as I argue that her skin and hair are the victims of her poor diet, it is hard to get through to her. One day she asked me to talk to her pet snake who was refusing to eat. "His skin even looks dull and pale," she agonized. I knew the answer before I even asked. Animals reflect their owners until we pay attention and do something about it.

Our pets care about us and want to show us our self-destructive behaviors. When an animal has blood sugar issues or liver problems, I check if the owner abuses alcohol. When the animal has respiratory issues, I check if the owner smokes. If the animal seems confused, lethargic, or disorientated, I check if the owner is abusing drugs, prescription or otherwise.

The good news is we can tell our pets that we acknowledge the issue and are working on it. This will usually solve the animal's issue. Of course we can't help many of our health ailments, and our pets are there to guide and support us.

If you are feeling guilty about this, don't be too hard on yourself. Your animal chose this purpose and wants this job in life. They love you and their role as a healer. Also, not every ailment they have is from you. Animals also bring their own illnesses and eventually their physical body may wear out as well. They get old just like us, so don't forget, aging is natural. The point is just to pay attention to your health, your emotional energy, and do your part in keeping your pets healthy, too.

Signs that you may have a healing animal

They come around to be petted when
you feel down or stressed.

When you have an ailment, they have a similar ailment.

You feel better when you stroke your pet and
when they are near you.

Taking care of your healing animal

If you have a stressful job, decompress before
you come home and pet your animal.

When they have an ailment, look to yourself.
Could this be a message for you?

Make sure they have fresh, clean water to
help them process negative energy.

Remember to thank them for their role.
They like to be appreciated.

CHAPTER 12

Happy Pets

The question I get asked more than anything is "Is my pet happy?" Most pet owners want to know what their animal is thinking because they want to make sure they are happy. Pets also want to make their owners happy and are at their most content when they feel they are loved and appreciated. Having good communication between pet and owner often solves many misunderstandings and this makes everyone happy.

Pet Peeves – The Main Complaints

There are several complaints that seem to come up over and over again in my animal communication sessions. The following are some of our pet's main pet peeves. The animal kingdom is loving me for this!

No companion – Most animals naturally live in groups and like to have company most of the time. If they are left alone they can get depressed, stressed, lonely, and bored. For example, horses need a stablemate, even if it's another type of animal, as they are herd animals and don't like to be alone. Many dogs and cats prefer a friend as well. Although some animals are an exception to this, preferring the alone time they have with mom or dad and don't want any competition for their affection. Be sure to tune in and ask your pet if they would like a companion. If you do introduce another pet, be sure that their personalities are compatible.

Can't go outside – Most animals love the outdoors. They need the exercise, fresh air, and the opportunity to explore. Sometimes you may be afraid to let a cat or a small dog outside due to dangers in their surroundings. Most animals have told me that they prefer to risk the dangers and enjoy themselves. However, there has to be some give and take here. Perhaps you can compromise and make them a safe outdoor space on an enclosed balcony or catio (patio for cats). If they cannot go out, make sure you have lots of green plants inside. (Make sure the plants are animal-safe and not poisonous.)

Don't go on walks. Tied up all day – Animals love to be taken out by their owners. Dogs need their exercise and to run. Make sure they get plenty of this. This is more important for certain breeds than others. If you plan to get a very active young dog, make sure you have the time to give them the exercise they need. Sometimes an animal will even come into your life because you are the one who needs the exercise!

Cat bells – Cats often complain to me about bells attached to their collars. They love to stalk and hunt and this just kills the fun! (Although I'm sure the birds and mice would have another opinion!) Be sure your pets like their collars and anything else they wear and that it fits safely and properly.

Cats not allowed to hunt – Although we see a cat catching a mouse or a bird as something terrible, it is their nature. Yes, I have a hard time with it and I run to rescue the lizards from the dog and the birds from the cat. But if it happens when you're not around, don't be too upset with your pet. On a higher level of consciousness, remember the bird or the lizard chose that experience. They know they can reincarnate easily and quickly.

Don't like the new boyfriend/girlfriend – Our pets have opinions about our new partners and friends, and sometimes they can get quite jealous. Make sure you give your pets lots of extra attention if you have a new person in your life who takes up your time. And remember, they are also very perceptive so check in with your pets to see what they are thinking. If they don't like your new boyfriend, perhaps you should listen!

Mom/dad won't listen to my advice – Often they complain that they are giving you messages and advice, but you are not listening. It can be very frustrating for them that they can hear us and we usually can't hear them. When you do communicate and they give you advice, pay attention and don't just ignore them.

Mom/dad tells me to do something and then gets mad at me when I do it – Make sure your thoughts match what you want them to do, not what you don't want them to do. When they see a particular behavior staying in your thoughts, they presume that's what you want them to do (even though it may actually be a bad behavior that you are fearful of them doing).

Variety of food – We would get bored with the same kind of food everyday. Make sure your pets get a variety of nutritious foods. Cats and dogs love to have things like raw meat (served room temperature) and other healthy treats. You can ask your pets what foods they like and also what is good for them. Be careful though that they are not telling fibs to get some tasty treats. (Be sure to confirm any dietary changes with your vet.)

Boredom – Sometimes animals simply get bored. Make sure your pet has plenty to do, as well as lots of playtime. If they like toys, make sure they have a variety. But most of all, they want lots and lots of attention.

Moving – Moving can be very scary. Send your pet messages about what to expect well before the moving day itself.

Animals next door. Territorial cats and dogs – There is a whole neighborhood dynamic going on that you may not know about. Be aware of the other animals in the neighborhood and your pet's reactions to them.

Peace not war – Animals are peaceful and loving. Normally they would do anything to keep the peace. They really don't like it when you raise your voice or get upset with them. If they exhibit a behavior that upsets you, try to communicate with them in a calm, more reassuring way than yelling or becoming angry.

Don't have a job. Don't know my place – Animals love to feel useful. Make sure you assign them a role and tell them how good they are at it. This is especially important if you have more than one pet in your home.

Love, love, love – Animals can never get enough love and attention from mom and dad!

Keep Them Informed

Often a pet just wants to know what is going on. Perhaps they have heard little snippets of information about something that will happen in the future, but they don't have the full picture and are concerned. Let them know about any major changes that are coming up. For example, a change in your job or routine, new animals coming to the family, a visit to the vet, moving, or visitors coming to stay.

Animals Can Tell Time

Yes, I'm serious, they can tell time! Don't ask me how they know, they just do! It's not that they are looking at the clock or anything. As I discussed earlier, it is their innate ability to tap into the Universal Consciousness. Do you ever wake up just a few minutes before your alarm goes off? This is you being in tune with your internal clock and putting out to the Universe what time you need to wake up. Animals are much more in tune with this skill than we are.

Some animals don't care that much about time and schedules. But if you have a pet who tends to get anxious when left alone, they may feel better if they have a schedule and know exactly what is going on and when. You can give them a lot of reassurance simply by telling them your schedule.

If you tell them when you are coming home from work, they will understand you. You could specifically say the time that you will be home (e.g., 5:30 PM) or tell them you'll be back just before the sun goes down. Through your thoughts, show them to be relaxed. Make sure you are not anxious when you do this. If you are feeling anxious about them being anxious, they will likely pick up on this and that's how they'll act.

Usually this is temporary and only lasts until you leave. It is a little like when you drop your child off at daycare. The child cries and makes a fuss, and the parent feels terrible. However, the moment the parent has left, the child has already moved on to playing with their toys and is no longer crying. Animals can be similar. They make a huge fuss as you leave and they become anxious (mostly from picking up on the owner's anxiety), but once you are gone, often they are perfectly fine.

Sometimes if an owner stays anxious all day, continuing to worry about leaving their pet, the animal will sense this and will stay anxious as well. Perhaps they may even think that their owner wants them to be anxious which can only lead to a stressed pet. If you can, try to always send your animals the message that you are calm and everything is fine, even when you aren't with them or have left them alone.

Letting your animal know what time you will be returning is a very easy way to keep them calm. If you give the message that you are coming home at 4 PM, they actually understand this and will be expecting you. However, if 4:15 PM rolls around and you're still not home like you said, they may get anxious. They were perfectly fine until the last 15 minutes, which may be the time your couch cushion gets chewed to shreds.

Prepare Them in Advance

Whenever there is a change or an event in their life that they might be anxious about, prepare them. If they have a trip to the vet, let them know when and what is going to happen. If you are planning on moving to a new home, let them know as soon as possible. Tell them when and visualize where you will be going. They can get very worried if they see boxes packed and they are only able to pick up little snippets of information. If you are going out of town, tell them how many nights you will be gone, what time you will be back, and who is going to take care of them. The more you can tell them, the calmer and better behaved they will be while you're gone.

I live in a hot, fire zone in the Los Angeles National Forest. Luckily none have ever come over our property, but I once had a really close call. A large forest fire was out of control and headed right toward us. The Sheriff's Department came and ordered an evacuation. I had several horses that needed to get on a trailer to take them to a safe location. Two of them were quite young and scared of trailers. The one other time I'd attempted to load them on a trailer, even my experienced horse wrangler friend couldn't persuade them. Now it was an emergency and they had to be loaded within the hour.

My friend was on his way to wrangle the horses. I was safely elsewhere with my cats, dogs, guinea pig, and other rescues. I sat quietly and sent messages to the two young horses, imagining them walking gently and slowly straight onto the trailer. Then I got the instinct to talk to my old pony. "I have a job for you," I told him. I explained how there was a fire coming and everyone needed to stay calm. I needed my old guy to talk calmly to the others and show them the way. Later my friend called, very relieved. "I couldn't believe it. I put the old pony on first, and the two babies just walked straight on behind him!"

Keeping Your Pet Happy

Feed them a variety of foods that they like.

Make sure they get lots of fresh air and exercise.

They love playtime with mom or dad.

They love to be appreciated.

Make sure they know what is expected of them.

Let them know what is happening in the future.

Love, love, and more love.

Remember to thank them for their role.
They like to be appreciated.

CHAPTER 13

Behavioral "Problems"

Sometimes an animal will start to exhibit a behavior that is out of character. If your pet is suddenly soiling the carpet, chewing things, or acting up in a way that is unlike them, they are almost certainly trying to get your attention. Even if your pet has been doing a particular behavior for a long time, tuning in and talking to them about why they are doing it can often solve the problem.

Animals want to be good, make you happy, and win your love. There is almost always a reason they are doing something. Though be prepared, sometimes it is something you are doing or not paying attention to, and you may be the one who needs to change.

To Ask an Animal Why They Do a Behavior

1. Follow the steps to connect.
2. If this is not your own pet, start with easy questions that you can confirm with the owner to verify the connection.
3. Continue with light conversational questions (e.g., favorite activity) to be sure the animal is comfortable and at ease.
4. Now ask them about the behavioral issue their owner has identified and get their side of the story.

5. Make sure a health issue is not causing the behavior.
6. Once you have discovered the issue, it may be resolved simply by understanding why the animal is exhibiting this behavior.
7. If it is something the animal does not want to change, look for a compromise or negotiate a bribe/incentive. Find out if there is a favorite treat or activity you can use as this incentive.
8. If you make deal with the pet, make sure their owner is willing to agree and follow-through on their end!

Whose Behavior Do We Need to Change?

Often clients come to me about a behavioral problem that turns out to not be a problem at all, but simply a misunderstanding. The animal will often explain how the behavioral issue is caused by something the owner is doing, and the animal is either protesting or trying to bring light to the matter. Usually this can be resolved by simply understanding the situation. Often it turns out that the owner needs to change in some way. In almost all cases there is a "legitimate" reason that an animal is acting out. Usually it is lack of attention, lack of exercise, jealousy, being locked up all day, being confused about a situation, not knowing their role in the family, being a mirror of the owner's own actions, or trying to alert the owner about a health issue. Sometimes it is just inconsistency on the part of the owner and their pet gets confused or even irritated.

If a compromise needs to be made, the animal may agree to stop doing the offending behavior in return for a special treat. More often than not, the special treat that they want is more attention from mom or dad.

Some behaviors may have developed because of experiences they had before they came to be your pet. Many of our animals are rescues and we don't know their history. This doesn't mean that you cannot correct these behaviors. Through communication they can inform you about their past experiences, and you can more easily convince them not to be afraid anymore.

Some behaviors may be related to the breed or type of animal.

In this case it is instinctive and may be a little more difficult to overcome. However, with patience and communication, most problems can be resolved.

The following are potential areas to consider when solving behavioral issues:

Mirroring the owner – Often our animals mimic us. If we are stressed, anxious, or lashing out, our animals may act in the same way.

Variety of healthy food – Do you take care that they are fed consistently and are given healthy food and fresh clean water? Also, their food can become boring so a little variety sometimes is nice.

Plenty of exercise – Dogs need to go outside and run. Cats love playtime as well. Even snakes and other reptiles need a big enough cage to get exercise or their growth may be stunted and they can become aggressive.

Bathroom access – Are your animals locked up for long periods of time? Make sure they have access to the outside. If they don't, make sure someone can take them out at reasonable intervals. For cats, be sure to keep their litter box clean. Caged animals also need their cages cleaned regularly.

Playtime – Make sure they have enough playtime and attention. This can be their exercise time as well. Provide them with toys to play on their own, but more importantly, find activities that you love to do together.

Love time – Be sure to spend time giving your pets love and affection. Stroking a pet is very beneficial for you as well as for them.

Keep them healthy – If an unusual behavior occurs, make sure that it is not caused by a health issue. Sometimes an animal will call out for your attention when it is ill.

Jealousy – Could your pet be jealous of a new animal, visitor, new baby, new relationship, or someone else they may feel is receiving more of mom or dad's attention.

Changes in the household – Are there changes happening in your home or at work? Is your pet confused about something taking place in the home? Let your pet know about upcoming changes before they happen.

Not getting along with others – If you have multiple pets are there difficulties between them? Make sure each animal has its own role in the household.

Consistency – Do you allow your pet to do an activity at some times but not at other times? Make sure your message is clear. Confusion can be a source of stress for your pet.

Common Behavioral Issues

Bathroom Issues

One of the most common behavioral issues I hear about is when an animal is going to the bathroom in an inappropriate place (e.g., on the carpet or not using their litter box). If this is a sudden change in behavior, it is a strong indication that something occurred and there is a specific reason for this unusual behavior.

First rule out any medical issues. Make sure your pet doesn't have a urinary infection, kidney problems, or some other health issue. Then see what changes have taken place. Does the animal feel more attached to one family member? For instance, if the dog feels like it is mom's dog and mom and dad get into an argument, the animal could be trying to protect mom and mark his and mom's territory. An animal could also simply be looking for attention or be upset with you for some reason.

Look at what has changed recently in the family and particularly with the person the pet feels most attached to. Could the pet be a mirror for that person? For example, is that person "pissed off"? (Note the word and its connotation.) Is there a new animal or baby in the home? Could it be attention they want? Are you being consistent or do you change what you are asking of them? Do you keep their kitty litter in the same place and keep it clean? Are they able to go outside or is it because they simply cannot hold it in so long? Are you moving or stressed at work? Even if you have only talked about it outside of the home, remember they still know!

Your animal is trying to tell you something by soiling. Dogs and cats especially will exhibit this behavior when they are trying to get their message across. Although horses are known to deposit their manure in their own feed bucket when they are annoyed with us or bored. Specifically note when the bathroom issues are occurring and what has changed at that time.

Joey & Judy

Judy came to see me because her cat had suddenly started pooping in her bathtub of all places. There were cat litter boxes available, and he never had a problem before. All of a sudden, he took a liking to the bathtub. As I tuned in to the cat, I saw Judy's new boyfriend coming over to her apartment. I felt that his emotions were pretty cold and distant. Judy was desperate for love in her life, and this guy was taking advantage and using her. Judy just kept hoping to hear the words, "I love you." This never happened; the guy was bad news. All this was according to her cat, Joey, who knew his mom very well.

But why the bathtub? Well, whenever the boyfriend was coming over, Judy would spend hours in her bathroom, sprucing herself up for the date. Judy needed to resolve her relationship with her boyfriend. This little therapy session with her cat got Judy out of a horrible relationship. Judy now has a wonderful guy in her life and Joey keeps to his litter box.

Samantha & Sara

Samantha's little Pomeranian, Sara, had always been housetrained and had never soiled the carpet. All of a sudden, Sara started to poop in the bedroom and the hallway. I asked Samantha what had changed. All she could think of was that her sister had been visiting with her two cats.

When I tuned into Sara, she relayed two things. First she tried to convince me the poop was not hers at all but rather from the cats. I knew this was not true. Was she trying to get the cats in trouble? Yes, absolutely! The second thing she revealed was that Samantha's husband, Dave, was a "cat person" and he only tolerated Sara. Sara was worried that Dave would decide to adopt cats after being around these two and seeing how cute they were. Sara wanted to make sure Dave really didn't like the cats.

As soon as Samantha understood the situation, she spent time with Sara expressing how special Samantha thought she was and that she would never be replaced. Rather than trying to get Dave to talk to Sara, it was easier for Samantha to convince her that Samantha would make sure nothing ever happened to her.

Vicky & Her Cats

Vicky had several cats. Not only did she have her own brood of cats, but several neighborhood strays hung out in her yard as well. All of a sudden some of her cats started peeing in the house. Nothing much had changed so she couldn't figure out what the problem might be. When I tuned in, I saw her house. It was a very old house, probably over a hundred years old. They showed me a hallway and the particular room where they were peeing. But why?

I saw an older lady in spirit occupying this space as well as Vicky and her family. This particular ghost had been a cat lover in her era. In fact, I'd say she had been a bit of a cat hoarder. Along with this old lady spirit were many cats in spirit. Vicky's cats were being territorial with this huge brood of cats that Vicky couldn't actually see. I prescribed a good ghost clearing of the house so the lady in spirit could move on along with her cats.

Arguments Between Animals in the Family

Animals like to feel helpful. When an animal feels like they don't have a role, it can make them confused, despondent, or even irritable. This is especially important when you have a multiple pet household. They may fight with each other for your attention or when they feel like another animal is doing *their* job. Make sure your animals are appreciated for their job. Tell them things like, "You are my healing dog and I really appreciate what you do for me" or "You are my wise cat and I know you help me with little intuitive thoughts."

When you have multiple animals, make sure they each have their own individual role. Also make sure your animals are clear what their role is and that they feel appreciated for it.

Barking

Barking is one of the hardest habits to break. Very often dogs feel that they can't help themselves. Remember, each animal has two parts: their higher consciousness nature and their instinctive nature. Barking is instinctive and it can take a lot of restraint on their part to stop. So even if you get the message across to them, they still have to exercise a lot of self-control to follow-through.

If they feel like they have the job of "protector," make sure you tell them that you feel secure and protected, and they don't need to bark anymore. Be sure to visualize them being calm. So when the postman is coming up your street, don't think, "Oh no! He's going to run at the door barking." I want you to think, "He's being so calm and has such good self-control." Remember, they are listening to your thoughts and mimicking what you are thinking.

Use positive words not negative ones. If you say, "Stop barking" or "Don't bark," they only hear the word "bark" and not the word "don't." Instead tell them, "Be calm" and make sure your demeanor is feeling and thinking "calm."

Bribes or incentives are also very useful. When your pet is being very good, especially when it is a situation where in the past they would have barked, remember to reward them with what you agreed upon. Also make sure they are getting outside enough and getting lots of exercise.

Even with the best of communication, you are still dealing with the animal's instinctive nature. No matter how much they understand and try to be good, sometimes they just can't help themselves. Some firm but loving training techniques may need to be utilized along with communication and understanding so that you can help your pet overcome their instinctive behavior.

Wrecking the House

Animals sometimes chew or tear up the furniture when they are left alone and get anxious abut where you are. Make sure you tell them how long you are going to be gone and where you are going. They can tell the time, so give them the specific time that you will return. If you are going to be late, send a telepathic message letting them know. Make sure your thoughts are on them being good and not on them chewing the couch. Remember, they hear your thoughts and do what they think is being asked of them. Perhaps they are simply trying to get your attention because they have a message and you haven't been listening. Talk to them and find out what they want to tell you.

Snapping or Biting

Sometimes snapping or biting is related to something that happened before your pet came to be yours. Communicating with them about why they do a particular behavior can help you to know how to proceed. Are they doing this out of fear of being attacked? Are they aggressive because of poor handling? For example, perhaps they were kicked or badly treated by a man wearing big work boots. Now they are fearful and go after all men with big work boots. Maybe a toddler inadvertently hurt them because they didn't understand or know any better and now they snap at children. Even if there is a justified reason, this is still not acceptable behavior.

Start by talking with your animal about why they are snapping or biting. If they are afraid, you need to convince them that they are now safe and that you will protect them from it happening again. Still, it is an ingrained reaction and you are going to have to work patiently and consistently with them. Reinforce how happy you are when they have the opportunity but are able to keep themselves from snapping or biting. They are like children in that they love to make us happy and crave our praise and appreciation. Always hold the image of them doing the proper behavior rather than what you don't want.

Even with the best communication, you are still dealing with the animal's instinctive nature. Many times dogs that are aggressive need to have a human they can look up to as their pack leader. If communicating alone does not solve the problem, you may need to use an animal trainer to help them relearn and modify their instinctive behavior.

Chewing, Scratching, and Digging

Sometimes these behaviors are to get your attention, especially if they are new behaviors. Do they get enough exercise and attention? They could simply be bored. Make sure when you take something away from them that you give them a replacement. So when you take away your shoes, replace them with a chew toy and say, "This is good for you to chew on."

Sometimes chewing and scratching could be related to anxiety. If this is the case, make sure they are informed of when you will be home and what is going on. Also make sure you are consistent with your discipline. For example, do you allow them to scratch the curtains but dad does not? This could be very confusing to them. Although it is less likely, check their teeth and claws to make sure there are no medical issues.

If they are digging up your flowerbeds, show them a better place to dig. Make it a fun game and join them in digging in an appropriate area. Perhaps you could bury a nice bone there. Be sure to send them a visual image of them digging in the appropriate area and reward them when they do.

Dangerous Behavior

Sometimes an animal's behavior can be dangerous, such as chasing cars or running across the road. Show how much you love them and what could happen if they run into the road. Although it may seem graphic, if you visualize and show them that it wouldn't be pleasant if they got run over by a car, they really get the message.

If they have wandered from home before, talk to them about the dangers. Perhaps wild animals live in your neighborhood. Tell them about coyotes, for instance. Even other cats and dogs protecting their territories can be terrifying to a pet who wanders off at night. Emphasize how comfortable and happy they are at home with you.

Understanding and Resolving Issues

Fears

Sometimes an animal will tell you they do something because they are afraid. Usually this is due to an incident in their past that caused this fear to develop. Ask the animal what the incident was and see if you can reassure them that this won't happen again. Oftentimes this can be the solution.

I had a horse who hated water. She would not jump the water jumps and was even fearful of a puddle on the ground. When I tuned in, I saw an incident with an old owner who whipped her to make her cross a puddle of water. She slipped and had gotten really scared. A short animal communication session and telepathic reassurance was much quicker and easier than trying patiently again and again to "train" her to jump over water. I was able to visualize sending the message that water jumps were fun and easy, and the training part went much easier.

Be Conscious of Your Thoughts

Your animals do not "listen" to what you say; they hear your thoughts, which are conveyed through emotions, visual images, and thought patterns. Sometimes we say one thing while projecting a completely different image or feeling. If you are asking them to do something, make sure you are visualizing it in a positive manner. Focus on the behavior you want rather than the behavior that you fear they may do. For example, if you are trying to get them to stop jumping on the couch, visualize them lying nicely in their doggie bed. Do not visualize your worry of them being on the couch. You may be inadvertently sending them this image, which they may interpret as what you want them to do.

Our animals are constantly picking up on our thoughts. They perceive what we say, not from our actual words, but rather from our feelings and our "thought packets." Every emotion, every daydream, every visual thought in our mind is constantly being projected, just as if we were talking to our pet constantly. If we are having a calm, civil conversation with someone but underneath we are seething with anger, the animal only picks up on the anger. Have you ever said things like, "I don't know why he doesn't like that man" or "I don't know why she runs away whenever they come over. They seem really nice." Your animal knows when a person is putting on a false front or if the person's real objective is hidden from us. Take note–if your dog doesn't like your new partner, perhaps you should look a little more closely at your relationship. They can see things we can't!

They say animals pick up on our fear. This is true because they can sense not only our thoughts, but the emotions that accompany them. Animals know exactly what you are thinking, so it is very hard to fool them. When we are afraid, we actually create an energy around us that has the vibration of fear. It is a complex mixture of thoughts and feelings, and animals can pick up on this energy. In fact, we may be so afraid that we actually trigger hormones in our body. Since animals have a very sensitive sense of smell, they can literally smell fear. Since you cannot hide your thoughts, you need to make sure you have your emotions in check when dealing with animals.

"But She Told Me to Do That..."

My sister-in-law in England asked me about her new dog, Murphy. Murphy was a rescue so she didn't know his history. She and my brother had taken the dog for a long walk in the country. They went to a beautiful area about five miles away, but when it was time to leave, Murphy didn't want to go. He absolutely wouldn't get into the car. Every time they tried to pull him into the car, he would slip out of his collar and run off.

My brother happens to be a very athletic runner and decided he would simply run home with Murphy. They ran all the way–the entire five miles. The next time they took him, the exact same thing happened. Once again, my brother ended up having to run home with Murphy. They wanted to take Murphy to even further places for walks, but my sister-in-law was too afraid that they still wouldn't be able to get him into the car. Would my brother then have to run back even further than five miles? They wondered if Murphy had been hit by a car or had some other traumatic experience in a car.

I tuned in. After getting a little confirmation on his personality, I asked him about his previous home. He hadn't had the best life to date but nothing with a car that I could see. So then I asked him why he wouldn't get into the car. "But she told me to do that!" he insisted. "She told me to slip out of my collar and to not get in the car. Then she told me dad would have to run home five miles with me. And, oh, it was soooo much fun!!"

I asked my sister-in-law what exactly she had been *thinking* as she tried to catch Murphy. She admitted that she had been worried all along and was thinking Murphy might not get into the car. She had even thought that he might slip his collar and wouldn't it be terrible if Murphy wouldn't come and dad had to run all the way home for five miles!

I instructed her to stay very calm the next time and think about how perfectly behaved Murphy was going to be. She should think that Murphy was going to get right into the car and enjoy the car ride home. Guess what? Next time he was much better.

So be very careful to project the thoughts and images of what you want and not what you are afraid you might get!

Negotiating a Deal

Once you have determined what the issue is, a compromise may be needed between the owner and the animal. One of the most important facets of behavior modification can be negotiating a deal with the animal. If they don't want to alter their behavior, this might be the best way to convince them. Follow-through is imperative for this to work. Whenever you negotiate a deal, make sure that the owner will keep their promise. An example of a negotiated deal is "I'll walk you more if you don't dig under the fence."

Punishing

Never hit or shout at an animal. This does more harm than good. We don't realize how much they may be affected by our shouting at them, as their depth of emotion is so much more than we realize. Talk to them and let them know what they did wrong because they will understand you. Putting them in a "time out" is also a more effective training tool than yelling. Tell them, "You did something I didn't like, so I am going to put you in a time out for 10 minutes." I don't believe you have to catch them in the act for them to understand.

A New Pet with Behavioral Issues

When you are choosing a new pet, you can use your animal communication skills to tune in and find out about their history. This is especially useful if your animal is a rescue who you know has been mistreated. You can use your communication skills to reassure them and help them to trust that you won't hurt them. It can also help to make sure you are both on the same page about fixing any behavioral issues together. This combined with lots of love can make all the difference.

Training an Animal

Unfortunately animal communication isn't a replacement for training. Don't think that you can telepathically tell your pet to go to the door and pick up the newspaper. You can't tune in and tell your pet to spin around three times, sit, and then give you their paw. It doesn't work that way. Believe me I tried when I first learned to communicate! In training you are working with their conscious mind to ask them to do something. In animal communication you are working with their higher self. Animal communication is working on a different higher plane with more purpose than that of training a pet to "fetch."

The best training incorporates what would be the animal's natural upbringing in the wild. Using a mixture of animal communication, explaining what you feel, as well as traditional training works wonderfully. In this way you are setting them up through communication to accept and understand the training they will receive.

For example, when training a dog, incorporating the natural order of the pack keeps the dog confident and happy but obedient. They feel safe under your leadership. You are their leader, their protector, as well as their friend. Traditional training works by mimicking the guidance they receive in the wild. You can communicate with them that you are a reliable pack leader and will protect and watch over them while giving them all the love and attention they need. Some habits that are instinctive and ingrained, such as barking or biting, may need some traditional training as well as your communication skills. After all, they may understand and want to please you on a higher level, but when that postman comes up the driveway, their instinctive self takes over.

You can use animal communication to help them be more relaxed and confident while training them. Use it to express that you are happy with them, which certainly aids in the "training" of a pet. It can also help them to understand what you want.

When riding my horse, I try to show him images of what a relaxed and wonderfully smooth ride we are having. However, we both have to put in hours of practice to "train" our minds and our physical bodies until this becomes instinctive. Animal communication alone is never going to make me a good rider who does well at horse shows. It's a combination of the right messages, visualization, and lots of practice. Of course, the trick is to be able to keep myself confident and relaxed so I can communicate that with my horse. It is almost impossible to fool them when they are so intimately in tune with us.

I believe that animal communication can be a great aid to training and that traditional training is wonderful and sometimes very much needed. In general, though, communicating with an animal is on a higher plane and quite different from traditional training.

Common Behavioral Issues

Bathroom issues – What has changed in your household? Are they marking you or their territory? Are there other animals they are keeping at bay? Are you upset with someone?

Multiple animal disagreements – Are they sure of their role in the family? Do they each get enough attention?

Barking – Are they getting enough attention? Do you tell them you are grateful for their protection? Do you think negative thoughts about their barking? Are they getting exercise? Can you negotiate a deal?

Snapping or biting – Are they afraid? Are they asserting their authority? Do they know their role in the family? Can you convince them not to be afraid? What are you thinking? Can you negotiate a deal?

Chewing objects – Are they anxious about you leaving and, if so, have you told them when you will be returning? Did you check their teeth? Do they have toys to play with? Can you negotiate a deal?

Digging holes – Have you assigned a place where it is ok for them to dig? Are they getting exercise? Why are they doing it? Is there a place that it would be ok for them to dig?

Fears – What are they really afraid of? Can you make it safe for them? Are you being anxious? Have you given them a schedule if they are afraid of being alone?

Chasing cars – Have you explained to them what you are afraid of? Do you have the "wrong" thought in your head? Do they think they are protecting you by chasing the car?

Wandering off – Have you explained the dangers? Do you have good communication in case they get lost? Do they get to go outside enough?

Won't come when you call – Are you clear and calm when you call them? Do you expect them to misbehave? Do they get enough attention? Make sure they know this is not playtime.

CHAPTER 14

Tracking a Lost Pet

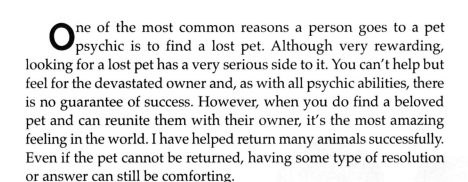

One of the most common reasons a person goes to a pet psychic is to find a lost pet. Although very rewarding, looking for a lost pet has a very serious side to it. You can't help but feel for the devastated owner and, as with all psychic abilities, there is no guarantee of success. However, when you do find a beloved pet and can reunite them with their owner, it's the most amazing feeling in the world. I have helped return many animals successfully. Even if the pet cannot be returned, having some type of resolution or answer can still be comforting.

You probably can imagine how distraught you might feel if your animal was missing. This is why I instruct my students to practice animal communication with their pets, just in case that day ever comes.

The following are the basic steps to find a lost pet:

1. Follow the steps to connect. Try not to allow any anxiety over the pet being missing to affect you when you are conducting a session.

2. If this is not your own pet, then start with easy questions that you can confirm with the owner to verify the connection.

3. Continue with light conversational questions (e.g., favorite activity) to be sure your animal is comfortable and at ease.

4. Ask if they feel hungry, thirsty, or are in pain. If they do feel any of these things, the good news is that having these issues means that they are alive.

5. Scan the animal's body to see if they are injured.

6. How do they feel emotionally? If they feel wonderful and very comfortable, they could be in a good situation, but they could also be passed over. Ask more questions to clarify.

7. Ask if there is anyone around them. The presence of a passed over relative is a distinct sign that they have passed.

8. Ask what they see. It may be darkness if they are hiding or trapped somewhere. If you don't see anything, start by using your imagination and allow the animal to correct you. Ask about their location, the smells, if any other animals are around, etc. Are they stuck somewhere? What are they afraid of? Other animals perhaps?

9. Ask what direction they went in when they left the house or the place they were lost from. Ask them to tell you step-by-step which way they turned and what they saw.

10. Ask if they want to come home and why they left. (Sometimes if an animal has left, it is because they may not want to come back.)

11. Ask your animal spirit guide and your loved ones in spirit to protect the animal until they can be found and to help guide you to them.

12. Set a time with the animal to go looking for them.

Lets go through the steps to find a lost pet in detail. You are going to be using all that you have learned about communicating and we are also going to be using remote viewing.

Find a quiet place where you won't be disturbed. Protect yourself and get into the communicating zone. You will be connecting in the same manner that you would for any other animal communication session.

Start to feel their personality and ask them some simple questions like, "What is your favorite treat?" This may seem inappropriate at this urgent time with a very anxious owner and a possibly frightened or injured pet. However, you need to make sure that you are definitely connected and you'll need the verification from the owner. I usually find that the owner gets a glimmer of hope when you start to give them details about their animal and you are clearly communicating. If this is your own pet, try to tune in and feel a familiar personality. Don't worry if you are not sure if you are connected, just trust and continue.

Now ask the animal where they are currently located. Imagine that you are looking through the animal's eyes. What do you see around you? Are you somewhere dark, perhaps hiding or trapped? Are you in an unfamiliar house or yard? If you can't see anything, ask what you smell, feel, and sense about the place.

If the animal is scared, hungry, or weak, reassure and comfort them. If the animal is giving you any of these feelings, it's a good sign. They are definitely still alive!

If your animal is telling you they feel warm, loved, and serenely peaceful, they may have passed over already. If you think this may be the case, then ask for other confirmation such as, "Who are you with?" If they describe the owner's mother who is already in spirit, then you have the answer. Ask them what the last thing they remember is. If they were hit by a car, it could be an image such as the headlights. As sad as this may seem, if this is the case, it is better that the owner be given the answer. If for some reason the owner was not supposed to know then the answer would not be given. Sometimes an animal may not want to tell you in order to spare their mom or dad the emotional grief. Just say what you receive even if you are telling the owner that you are not sure.

The animal may be perfectly happy and not hurt. They could have been rescued. Sometimes they will seem surprised that such a fuss is being made as they were just out on a little adventure. This attitude is most common among cats. See what you get at this point. Are they really lost? If so, did they run away? Were they chased by another animal?

Ask the animal to take you back to the moment they left their house or yard. Imagine that you are in the animal's body and leaving the property. Which exit did you take? Ask the owner if they recognize what is being described (e.g., if it is the front door, back gate). Ask the animal which way they went and to describe everything they see as they recall things, step by step. They will be describing it from their perspective (not what you as a person would describe). The following is an example from the animal's perspective. "I crawled under the white wooden fence and then was on the hard ground. I turned right. Two doors down I passed the big black dog's house. He has a scary bark, but he's tied up. I took a few more steps and on the left is a post and a stone. There are lots of [urine] markings from the morning walk dogs."

You are going to see the path from their eye level and will see what an animal would notice, such as smelly things and other animals. The path you are shown may be jumping over the back fence and from yard to yard or roof to roof, rather than on the street. I once tracked a lost tortoise and they see the world from a very different perspective than a cat, for instance.

Surprisingly, the animal may even know the names of streets, places, signs, and businesses. The animal cannot actually read, but they can access the Universal Consciousness to obtain this information when they are quiet and relaxed. Ask for as much detail as possible and work with the owner who will hopefully recognize the path their pet has taken.

How did they get to where they are now? They could have become disorientated along the way. For example, if the animal was chased by another animal, they may have been too scared to notice which way they went. Perhaps they were picked up in a car by a rescuer and only know part of their journey.

Try to get a description of where they are now. Again, they will be showing you from their eye level and using their senses.

Can they leave and come home on their own or is it safer for them to stay put? Sometimes an animal feels trapped and scared by other animals in the area. I find that neighborhoods are divided into territories, mostly by cats and dogs. Your cat may be afraid to move from under a house because there are cat territories on three sides and a dog on the fourth. Often they are afraid of crossing domestic animal territories during the day and then wild animals loom at nightfall, and they cannot find a safe time to escape.

Are they in one place or have they moved from place to place? Is someone feeding them? Have they been taken into a home? If so, what does your animal see in the house? What do the people look like?

Ask to see a map of the area or a bird's-eye view of the place using your psychic sense to tune in and do a remote viewing of the area. Use your imagination. If you had to guess and visualize a map, what do you think would be on it?

Try getting a map of the area and see if anything looks similar to what you have perceived psychically. Can you see a body of water they have described? Can you see a dog park or an open field? Is there a row of shops? I suggest that you do not look at a map until you have first received as much information from the animal as you can. If you start by looking at a map, it would give you a preconceived idea of the area and may confuse you as to which are the actual messages from the animal.

If you are familiar with using a pendulum, try using it over a map of the area. You can hold the pendulum over points on the map and ask it to move when you have the correct location. You can also find out your Yes/No signals and then ask questions such as "Are they north of this street?" (See Appendix A for detailed instructions on how to use a pendulum.)

Ask the animal if they can come home on their own or with a little telepathic help from you to direct them. Now that you have a feel for the area, maybe it is a location where it is safer to tell the animal to stay put and that you will come get them.

Arrange a meeting place and time with the animal. Ask the animal what time would be safe for them to come out of hiding (if they are hiding). Yes, it sounds strange, but they do know time. For example, you can tell them, "I think I know what street you are on. Come out and meet me at 3 PM."

The owner will go to the location and attempt to call the animal. It may be helpful to bring a bag of treats to noisily shake or a toy whose squeaky sound they would recognize.

If you do not find the animal on your first attempt, please don't give up. Post signs in the area where you thought the animal should have been. They may not have been able to come out of hiding when you were there.

I often try to tune in to other animals in the neighborhood and ask for their assistance. I also ask for animals in spirit to help. I may tell the local animals that if they help me, I'll make a donation to the animal shelter in gratitude for their assistance. Don't forget to follow through on the donation (or ask the pet owner to), when they are reunited.

I have many amazing reunion stories and will share a few examples:

Janet & Suzy

Janet called me about her cat who had been missing for over a week. All I knew about her was that she lived somewhere in a desert region of California. Right away, I attempted to connect with her cat and used my remote viewing to tune in.

First I described her cat and its personality, Janet's house, and the other animals in the home. I got an initial "S" for her name (her name was Suzy). Ok, now I feel like I'm getting a good connection with her cat. I then put myself in the body of Suzy, and I ask her to look around and show me what she sees. She is in a residential neighborhood but is totally disoriented. I ask her to stay calm and remember her steps from home.

She describes slipping out of the front door, turning right, and then another right. I feel myself going down the steps and onto the road. I make a right and walk to the corner where there is a frisky little black dog. He is quite friendly, but he's not allowed past the black iron fence. I see him peeking between the slats. Then I turn. There is a lamppost halfway down with many dog smells on it. I am giving Janet enough markings that she can confirm that the direction and area sounds correct, but she is skeptical. It seemed too far from home for her to believe that Suzy could be in the area I was describing. Nevertheless, I told her to post some flyers and ask around.

Suddenly Suzy announces to me, "There were pink balloons in the sky but now they're gone!" (The owner told me that in the desert there were often hot air balloons that passed overhead in the afternoon.) Suzy was distraught, "I tried to get back and I was using the balloons as a marker, but now I'm really lost and the balloons have gone."

So that afternoon Janet went off with her flyers and followed the directions Suzy had given. As she was putting up flyers, a guy stopped and said, "I think I saw your cat a couple of days ago." Janet didn't find Suzy that day, but at least there was a possible sighting of her cat alive! As she was leaving, she noticed the remains of a children's birthday party and some leftover pieces of pink balloon on a gate, but no Suzy.

The next day I tuned in again. Suzy describes picking through a dumpster at the back of a convenience store. "Not likely," Janet says. Apparently the only convenience store is several blocks away and across a main highway. However, when Janet went to the store, the owner reported that a cat was hanging around the night before. Janet showed him the picture and, yes, Suzy was recognized.

Elated, Janet calls me. She is sure Suzy is alive and close by. The third time I tune in, I ask Suzy to absolutely stay put because "mom is coming for you right now." Then I ask where she is. Suzy describes sitting under a yellow house, looking at a blue-gray shed. There is a gate with a lion's head on it and to her right is a large stretch of field with some overhead power lines. She says the first initials of the streets are "L" and "S" and they are girl names. Janet knows of a Laura Street in the neighborhood. I tell Suzy to stay put, that mom is coming at 3 PM and will have a can of cat food. She is to listen for mom and as soon as she hears the food can rattle, to run out.

At about 2:50 PM I get a clear, urgent message as Suzy pops into my mind. "Tell her about the boat! Tell her there's a blue boat in the driveway!" Could this be correct? I knew they were out in the desert. Why would there be a boat? Nevertheless, I called Janet. "I think I just got a message. I'm being told to tell you that there's a blue boat in the driveway!" Of course not quite believing it, I added, "Perhaps it's a car with a blue cover or something."

Janet calls me back about an hour later. She is beyond excited. "You are never going to believe this. I drove down Laura and turned by the field. I had never noticed the power lines before but there they were. Then the most amazing thing happened. As I turned the corner, I saw a sailboat in a driveway! It had a big blue cover over the sails. My heart was pounding. I couldn't believe it. As I pulled closer, I saw that it was a pale yellow house with a blue-gray shed. Then I saw the wrought iron gate with a big lion's head! As I approached the house, there was my little Suzy peeking out at me from underneath the house. And by the way, the nearest cross street was 'Sarah.' "

It was a beautiful reunion, and I was so excited to have helped. Although, I think I had a little help from the animals in the neighborhood, and I had Janet promise to make a donation to the local animal shelter.

Now what Janet didn't tell me, and thank goodness she didn't, was that she had already received a reading from another pet psychic. This psychic sadly told her that Suzy had passed away. Janet didn't believe her and didn't want to give up. I was the end of the line call.

Why had Suzy left in the first place? Apparently Janet had recently moved to the neighborhood, and Suzy had simply gone off exploring. On this particular day the birthday balloons had been her marker to find her way back home but when they suddenly disappeared, she became disoriented. As she tried to make her way home, she was inadvertently getting further and further away. We made an agreement. Suzy would still be allowed out (she was very worried she wouldn't be), but she promised never to go further than a few houses in either direction.

Nina & Pumpkin

I received a photo from Nina who lived on the East Coast. Her cat had been lost for several days. He was a beautiful, fat, ginger cat. As I tuned in to this sweet old guy, I got the name "Pumpkin." Perhaps that was an easy one, as he looked very much like one. Still, I confirmed his favorite treats and his adorable personality. I knew he was quite old and had failing health, especially his liver. Nina confirmed the vet had suspected liver failure.

As I asked him where he was, I expected that it being winter, he would be freezing cold outside somewhere. He was actually warm, cozy, and curled up in a ball. There was a lady lovingly taking good care of him. Pumpkin was sitting on her lap, being nicely stroked and pampered. I asked the lady who she was and received the message, "Aunt Miriam. Breast cancer." I asked Nina if she had had an Aunt Miriam who died of breast cancer. Nina was shocked. She confirmed that she did indeed have an aunt with that name who had recently passed away from breast cancer. But what did that have to do with her cat?

I explained what I was seeing. It was a sad moment, but we both knew. Pumpkin expressed that when his health was failing, he knew that it was his time. Like many other cats, he didn't want a fuss to be made at the end. He just wanted to go somewhere quiet to lie down until he peacefully crossed to the other side in his sleep. He wandered off alone to die in dignity.

Although it was a sad ending, Nina was comforted and grateful to know that he wasn't lost and hurt somewhere and that this was the way he wanted it. She loved her aunt and was comforted to know they were together. I knew that Pumpkin wanted to get this message to mom or I would have never have been told this. In fact, it was probably Pumpkin himself that somehow was able to prompt Nina to contact me. Even from the other side, our animals can sometimes still arrange to get messages to us.

Carla & Sampson

Carla called me in great distress. Her dog had gone out for his usual afternoon playtime in the backyard but when she called him for dinner, he was gone. When I tuned in, I found a cute pampered Shih Tzu. He loved to take baths, be groomed, and even have his nails trimmed. I asked to be transported into his body and to go back through his last steps from the house. A loud boom of thunder had spooked him and sent him fleeing. He took the usual route that he and his mom used when they went on walks. He described this daily route in great detail. He knew the dog three doors down very well. He would laugh at this big brown dog who snarled at him but was safely tied up. Then he'd stop for a good sniff at the large iron box on the corner. However, today he was at a dead run. Then his escape was cut short by a person in a white van who picked him up.

But where was he now? He described the inside of a family home and we suspected it could be far away. It was almost Halloween and Sampson said the house had a huge spider on the roof that was the size of the entire house.

Carla was instructed to place a flyer two blocks north of her house at a park by a yellow school. Sure enough, when she went to this location, there was a yellow school with a park next to it. She was also instructed to place an ad online. Carla went through the neighborhood looking for the house with a spider on the roof, but couldn't find such a house.

We arranged to talk the following day. Immediately, a small mutt with a patch over one eye came through. "Just tell her thanks," he said. Carla cracked up. Apparently when she was at the park putting up flyers, there was a lady trying to catch a stray mutt. Carla, being an animal lover, stepped in to help. The two of them together were able to catch him. The mutt appeared to have a severe infection in one eye and together, they took him to the vet. The lady Carla was helping wanted to adopt the mutt but couldn't afford the vet bill. Carla paid for his treatment and the stray mutt got a new home.

Carla also had exciting news of her own. She had received a call from a person who saw her online ad. They had found a Shih Tzu who sounded just like Sampson, and Carla was going to go over there later. I eagerly awaited her call.

What was to come surprised both of us, but not in the way you'd expect. Carla went to the address. It was a house hidden behind some apartments a little back from the street. As she turned the corner, she couldn't believe her eyes. There in front of her was a house with a gigantic spider covering the entire roof! She knew it was the house Sampson had described. However, there was to be another shock. The dog this family had rescued wasn't Sampson. It looked almost exactly like him, but it wasn't. The family couldn't keep their little rescue. Having a big heart, Carla agreed to take him and to try to find him a new home.

I tuned in again. This time I got a pink apartment building with children's toys strewn along the side. Sampson was being kept in a small, grassy, fenced yard. He could just see a white van in the driveway. But where was it? He didn't know. As luck would have it, Carla received another call from her ad. As she pulled up to the address, she saw the pink apartment building and her heart leapt. She knew it was the one I had described, but her happy reunion didn't happen. There was a Shih Tzu here, but again it was not Sampson.

The last time I spoke to her she still had not found Sampson but hadn't given up hope. There was a silver lining to all of this, however. Carla had opened a Shih Tzu rescue. In her search for Sampson, she had recued eight Shih Tzus and a couple other mixed-breed dogs and placed most of them in new homes. Did Sampson trick me? Was Sampson actually passed on when I first spoke to him? Was this his plan all along, to help other lost dogs in need? I don't know. We were told what we were supposed to know. Clearly the Universe works in mysterious ways and perhaps the animals do a little as well.

CHAPTER 15

They Know the Future

One of the things that absolutely shocked me when I first started communicating with animals is that they know what is going on, even when they are not present. In fact, they even know the future. Animals have told me about conversations that took place when they weren't even in the room. The first time I became aware of this was when a cat said to me, "… and I don't like the people mom works with. They're mean. You should have heard what that girl Laura said to mom in the office last week! She's a B****! And I mean worse than a female dog!!"

Not only do they understand our phone conversations and other things they hear us say, they even know what we are doing at work! I was even more shocked when animals started telling me about things that were going to happen in the future. What is wonderful is that we can tune in to our animals and ask them for advice. We can even ask them to see into the future for us!

Piano Cats

At an expo I gave a mini-reading to a lady who brought pictures of her cats. They were cute, giddy, little critters. They showed me all around their home. However, there was one room in the house they were not allowed in which they were ever so curious about. People were allowed in but never the cats. I knew most of the people were little girls because the cats showed me the little shoes all lined up outside the door.

The girls would first take off their shoes and then they would go inside with mom. The cats would sniff the little shoes with delight. Some shoes were there regularly and had familiar smells. Some were there just once in a while. All were delightfully fragrant and the cats looked forward to the visitors. Oh, but if they could just peek inside!

I described what the cats told me and I, too, was dying to know what was inside the room. "I'm a piano teacher!" she said laughing. "I teach mainly children and yes, I make them take their shoes off!"

Then the cats really surprised me. They showed me a flyer pinned on what looked to be a school bulletin board. Then they showed me rows of ballet slippers outside the piano room. "Tell mom she's not to worry. There will be lots of them." My client was stunned. She was worried about not having enough clients and had just posted a notice at a local ballet school!

Parakeet Business Advisors

I once read for a young man who had a pair of parakeets. They were very chatty and finished each other's sentences. They told me dad was single and gave me a little glimpse of their apartment. "You know my dad is always walking around the apartment talking to himself." I was shown a visual of my client rehearsing in the mirror. It was an image he would probably have cringed at my seeing if he had known.

"He is always saying, 'Should I do this? Should I do that? What should I do?' He could just ask us because we know!" Then they added, "I mean we couldn't tell him directly. We couldn't give him a direct answer."

"What do you mean?" I curiously inquired. They explained, "Well, let's say he says, 'Should I do this business deal with Bob or should I do it with Lenny?' We know! But even if he asked us, we are not just going to say 'Do the deal with Bob.' He wouldn't believe us. But we could show him a golden pumpkin sitting on the lawn. We could put that visual in his head." They continued, "Well, a couple of days later when Bob calls and says, 'Hey, do you want to talk about this business deal over lunch? I heard that the Golden Pumpkin restaurant is really good.' Then he'd know that he should do the deal with Bob. He got the sign."

This made sense to me. Spirit often communicates with us in this same way. Spirit doesn't always give an answer to us directly because we are constantly questioning, but Spirit may give us a sign. Somehow animals can connect into the Universal Consciousness, as well. It seems that the knowledge is out there in the Universal Consciousness for us all to connect to. We humans just have a harder time accessing it. Animals seem to be able to just go there and access that knowledge.

Fish Screensaver

I did a reading for a lady who had several cats. One of the cats had quite a bit of advice for mom about her business. The cat seemed to know a lot about her different projects and particularly what she was researching on her computer. Then the cat added, "By the way, I love the fish screensaver."

My client was astonished as her cat described each of the fish swimming on her screensaver. "But this computer is only at work!" she told me. I asked her cat how she knew this. The cat described a tall plant stand that leaned against the office wall directly behind her mom's desk. Apparently the cat would often lie on the top of this plant stand. But this cat was at home in the apartment when she was at work! Apparently not. Somehow the cat was able to wander out of body psychically and sit in the office looking over mom's shoulder. What was even stranger was that my client said she sometimes actually felt the cat's presence behind her!

Asking for Advice

As crazy as it may sound, go ahead and ask your animal for advice about your business, relationship, or other matters. It can't hurt to see what advice they may give you. Make sure to look for the signs after you ask. Notice what comes up over the next few days. Does someone happen be talking about something related to your question? Do you notice an article on the Internet? Be open to receiving the signs.

Follow the same steps to connect as you would with another person's pet. You can either use a photo or have the animal be present. Trust that you are connected because you cannot verify this with a third party.

Ask your pet for help with a career choice, relationship decision, or life issue. When you are looking for an answer or insight, it is unlikely you'll be told straight out. What is more likely to come is some kind of sign. Over the next few days, pay attention to things that happen and what doors open for you. Grasp all opportunities presented to you, especially those that are unusual or synchronistic.

Give your pet a treat after the session. Remember to acknowledge their help and thank them. Heal your animal often with protective white light, especially those who help with healing and absorb stressful energies.

Our animals very much want to be our partners in life. That means that they are helping us in many more ways than we think. They place thoughts in our mind that we think are our own intuition, but often it is our animal guiding and directing us.

Henry

I once did a reading for Tom and his cat Henry. The young man had come with questions about Henry, his health, and his likes and dislikes. Tom got more than he bargained for. "Tell Tom he thinks he's writing a book." I repeated this verbatim. "Yes, I *am* writing a book," Tom asserted, a little surprised that I knew and a little indignant. Henry continued, "I'm the one writing the book! Tom needs to give me a little credit here!"

People are often surprised by what their animal knows about

them and this is not the only time that an animal has declared to me that they should get the credit for something. Our animals can literally go up to the universal knowledge bank and download information about our life, our purpose, and what is going on in our future. Perhaps one day we'll be able to do this just as easily as they can. But for now, isn't it useful knowing you have a little soothsayer in your home?

Our animals can not only guide us in our career choices and direct us on the path we wish to go, they also have a very good gauge on our new romantic partners. In fact, they already know what the probable outcome is to be.

Sonya's cats

Sonja was a cat lady and had quite the brood. The cats wanted the best for their mom and they knew she needed a human partner, as well. All they really wanted was for mom to be happy. Mom started dating Lou. She was very excited about him but hadn't yet brought him home to meet the family. Unbeknownst to Sonja, the cats knew him very well, even though they'd never met. They didn't need to. While Sonja was being swept off her feet on a date somewhere, her cats were not only listening, they knew Lou's backstory intimately.

It was time for Lou to be introduced. Sonja brought her man back to her apartment for a romantic dinner. The cats already knew that Lou did not have the best of intentions. He was more interested in Sonya's position at a film studio in town than in really getting to know her. Sonja knew that perhaps he had other motives, but she desperately wanted to believe it was true love.

The cats might have tried to show their mom that Lou wasn't being completely forthcoming and could have sent a little intuition her way. Perhaps they could have orchestrated a situation where Lou might have been caught showing his true colors. If that hadn't worked, they could have started acting out to get mom's attention. Maybe they would have peed on the carpet on date night or left cat hair on the dress she was to wear. Fortunately, they didn't have to resort to any of that. After dinner Lou plopped down on the couch and announced, "I'm allergic to cats." That was enough for Sonja to call it quits. "Yeah, don't let the door hit you on the way out," one of the cats said under his breath.

A few months later Lou was back on the scene, this time wooing one of Sonja's coworkers. Unfortunately this lady didn't have any cats at home to advise her and apparently she was taken for quite a ride.

Trust in the Connection

Our animals have been working with us for a long time, perhaps even many lifetimes together. Even when they are not physically around us, they are around us in spirit, always working with us and watching over us. When you understand this and really see them as your partner, you can experience a very deep relationship.

However, when we ask our animal partner to give us advice, it is not always clear. They are clear, but we often question it. It is more difficult to communicate with your own pet. Not that the connection is difficult, but it is difficult to trust that what you're getting isn't your own imagination.

With someone else's pet you can ask them questions for verification. With your own pet you just have to trust that the connection is there. Of course it feels like you are making things up, and you don't know if it is wishful thinking or a guess based on their personality. Confidence comes from practice. You need to develop confidence in your abilities by practicing on animals that you do not know.

Animals know what is happening in our life,
even when they are not present.

Animals are aware of our future and
potential possibilities.

Animals are able to tap in to the Universal
Consciousness and access universal knowledge.

We can ask our animals for help making decisions.

Animals are great evaluators of our relationship choices.

Our animals can put thoughts and intuitions into our
mind and help give us answers to our questions.

Animals have our best interests in mind.

We should give our animals more credit,
as they are our real partners in life!

CHAPTER 16

Past Lives, Future Lives

If you have ever loved an animal whom you have lost, you will agree this is one of the most painful experiences in life. What may make this slightly easier is to know that your pets can reincarnate and may even come back to you in this lifetime. Animals have much shorter life spans than we do and can choose to be with us multiple times in our lifetime. It is the same soul, the same personality but with different physical bodies. I have seen evidence of this in many readings. I have also experienced this firsthand with my own pets. I absolutely believe that animals reincarnate.

Reincarnation

After learning and experiencing animal communication, I feel more at peace with the loss of a pet. Nothing is the same as having your beloved pet with you physically to love and to hold, but knowing that they are around you in spirit and always there can be very comforting. Over and over again, I have seen confirmation that our pets stay around us and will even reincarnate to be with us again in our lifetime.

When our pets pass, I believe they remain with us in spirit. Some may reincarnate very quickly, and we suddenly find ourselves adopting a new loved pet. Others stay around us in spirit for a while and then reincarnate later. They always tell me that when it is their time to reconnect with us, they will let us know. You don't need to go searching for them in their reincarnated form. They will let you know and find you or give you a sign that they are here. This is why when you go to the local shelter and one particular dog looks at you in a familiar way, you just immediately connect. Perhaps someone shows up asking if you can adopt a kitten. Our pets find their way back into our lives. These are not coincidences.

Because an animal's lifespan is so much shorter than ours, they are able to reincarnate several times in our lifetime. In readings I have found this to be true over and over again. Many of our pets were also with us when we were younger. Have you ever thought that your cat reminded you of another one you used to have? Often their reincarnated self looks the same physically and may even have the same personality quirks.

People have many past lives as well. Just as you may recognize an animal that you had earlier in this life, you may also recognize them from a past life. Most animals that we feel strongly connected to have been with us not only in this life but possibly many other lives. Ask your animal how you have known each other in the past and see what interesting things pop into your mind.

I have found many examples of animals working with their owners through multiple lifetimes. I read for one lady who works with herbs and her cat would always patiently watch. In fact, she discovered that she had also worked with herbs in previous lifetimes in Switzerland, the Far East, and probably many other places. Her cat today would actually place images or intuitions into her owner's mind, helping her to recall information she had long since forgotten, but her cat could easily remember. This is why the cat would always watch her owner while she worked.

Sam & Mo

When I was about nine years old, I found a little stray kitten. I had heard a faint cry coming from behind a garden shed and there, under a piece of cardboard, I saw a pair of itty-bitty eyes looking back at me. He looked up at me, almost too weak to even meow, just the tiniest ball of fluff soaked through from a terrible storm. No one thought he would survive. I begged and begged my mom to let me keep him. Who could resist? It didn't take long for her to cave. I bottle fed him and pushed him around in my baby stroller. He grew to be a beautiful, healthy, black cat with two white paws. I named him Sam.

Sam loved canned baked beans. Although he wouldn't really eat them, he'd just suck off all the sauce and leave the beans. His favorite pastime was to swing on the curtains. He would stalk the window ledge back and forth, then turn away nonchalantly as if to give his victim a false sense of security. He would then quickly turn back to scare his imaginary prey and take a pouncing leap onto the curtain. Sam could run vertically from floor to ceiling up the curtains.

Many years later I had a cat named Mo who was black with two white paws. We rescued him from the pound. The story was that he arrived soaking wet and barely alive. I never would have considered them to be the same cat, but I kept calling him Sam for some reason. One day I set out some leftover baked beans. He came over very interested and licked off all the sauce but left the beans intact. "Strange," I thought. "Maybe it's a cat thing!" Then one day I noticed him stalking the curtains when he suddenly made a leaping pounce halfway across the room. As he went running vertically up the curtains, I knew why.

Major & Benny

Benny asked me to chat with his horse. Nothing was really wrong. Benny just thought it would be interesting to see what Major had to say. Right away, Major showed me the one thing that did bother him. "Do you have to be really careful around his face?" I asked Benny. "Major is telling me that he really hates any kind of cloth on his face, particularly near his eyes. He especially hates to have his eyes covered and wants you to be very careful about putting anything over his face."

"Wow, does he ever!" Benny replied. "Once when we won a horse show, they placed the winning ribbon on his bridle, and the wind made it flap over his eye. He literally reared up and bolted the other way. He'd never done anything like that before. He's normally so quiet and steady."

When I asked Major why he was so afraid, I saw a vision of a dark battlefield. Major was once again a very large, grand, bay horse. Benny was his rider then as well, although this time he was wearing battle armor. There were terrifying noises of clanking iron and other horses whinnying in fear. From out of nowhere, a man on a big black horse came charging toward Major. Suddenly Major couldn't see. The man had thrown something over his face and he spun around trying to shake it off, but couldn't. Major wanted to protect Benny, but he couldn't sense where he was or from what direction the adversary was attacking. Major spooked to the left, trying to rid the covering from his eyes.

As Major moved to the left, he felt another horse and rider crash into his side. Then I sensed a very distinct sad feeling as Major felt Benny go limp on his back. Benny had been hit from the left. If only Major hadn't spooked in that direction. If only he could have seen them coming. Major prayed that Benny could hang on as he took him to safety. However, it was too late and his limp body slid off into the mud.

Major was recalling a memory not from this life but from many centuries ago. It pained him even today. Major still couldn't forgive himself for what he thought was his error. This is why he hated to have his eyes covered.

I explained to Benny what Major was telling me. Benny was normally a comedian, and I was waiting for him to crack a joke in disbelief. Instead Benny went awfully quiet. Something had struck a chord with him. What's really strange is this. Benny pulled up his shirt to reveal a significant birthmark on his left side in the exact spot where Major said he took the blow. Both of us got chills when he showed me.

Benny spent time with Major thanking him and reassuring him this past life was in the past, and he had always been the best horse. I would like to say that Major's phobia about coverings around his eyes had gone away. It didn't, but Benny was a lot more understanding about it.

Cat in a Dog's Life

I find that in almost all cases, a bird reincarnates as a bird, a dog as a dog (usually even the same breed and physical characteristics), a cat as a cat, etc. Occasionally I find an animal who seems very human, but I don't think I have ever found an example of a person reincarnating as an animal. If your dog reminds you of your uncle or your grandmother, it's more likely that these people are around them in spirit.

Chemile

One of my strangest readings was for a cat. She was a beautiful, long-haired, all-white cat named Chemile. Chemile had a very regal air about her. "I am sure glad to be a cat again," Chemile told me. She explained that when her owner Emily was a young girl, Emily's mother was allergic to cats. Chemile had experienced many lifetimes as a cat with Emily. But in this lifetime Chemile had a dilemma. She couldn't come in as a cat because Emily's mother was simply too allergic. So when Emily was a little girl, in order to be around Emily and her family, Chemile had chosen to reincarnate as a dog. Chemile, who was now a cat, had been a dog when Emily was younger. Emily confirmed that when she was young she had a small, white, long-haired dog, and yes, Emily's mother was allergic to cats.

The Great Healers of Egypt

From time to time I come across cats who declare that they've had previous incarnations as a "Great Healer of Egypt." These cats are particularly self-important, often barely putting up with their subservient human owners. They are very serious, particular, and usually not interested in playful activities. They declare that they are wiser than we could possibly know. After all, once upon a time people came from far and wide to talk to them, a great healing cat. The humans were merely the assistant or conduit to bring these people in need and to speak their human language.

They often show me an image of their previous selves looking very large, almost panther-sized. I cannot quite tell if they were actually this large physically or if this is just a reflection of their extra-large persona.

From what I've been told, these great cats were healers and seers, prescribing herbs and other remedies. They tell me they were sought after and adored, even by the great pharaohs themselves. Those who "own" (haha, as if anyone owns them) one of these cats are often in the healing arts or have some great healing purpose themselves. Although the cat usually takes credit for their owner's healing abilities, psychic talents, and intuition.

During a reading, a client's cat told me that she had been a great Egyptian Healing Cat in a past life and that the then priest was her owner today. When I asked if the cat helped her owner in this former life, I was indignantly told that it was the other way around. She told me that she was the great healer of the temple and that the high priest was actually some kind of assistant to her. In this life the cat was continuing to work as a healer. What I find curious is that I have received many similar cat messages about this.

Pets who we feel close to are our soul mate. They can reincarnate again into our current lifetime and have probably been with us through many lifetimes.

CHAPTER 17

Animal Guides and Angels

Earlier we worked on connecting with your animal guide. Animals in spirit who are in other realms and dimensions are connected with us, helping us, and communicating with us. This includes our personal animal spirit guide, our own animals who have passed over, as well as other animal guides and angels. There is a whole world of these beautiful beings just waiting patiently to help us.

Animal Guides

We each have a main spirit guide assigned at birth to take care of us. This is usually a person who at one time was incarnated in our physical world. They have now evolved to the spirit realm and are extremely wise and loving. Then we have other guides who come and go throughout our life. For instance, a guide who may be with us for a short period of time to help us with something we are doing, learning, or to help us through a specific experience.

Just as we have guides who were once people, we also always have animal guides helping us. Usually we have several animal guides. These may be animals that lived on earth and have now passed over, or they may be animal energies from other times and dimensions. Some may be mythological creatures such as dragons or unicorns.

Often our animal guides are depicted in what we are drawn to or acquire, such as art or clothing. For example, a person might like to wear leopard print clothing or collect statues of frogs. These animal guides can be called upon to help us. Anytime we put our thoughts out to the Universe, these helpers are listening. Even more powerful is to meditate and call on these specific animals, asking them directly what you would like help with.

Seeing-Eye Bat

I made a connection with one of my animal guides about six months before I discovered my latent talents as a medium. However, at the time I hadn't really understood the significance of this event....

It was a hot summer night at the ranch and I had left my balcony doors open. I had woken up at about 3 AM and saw a bat fly into the bedroom. I'd seen birds and moths fly in before, but this was definitely a bat. It flew around the bedroom and then landed on top of an old painting with a large, ornately-carved wooden frame that was hanging over the balcony doors.

"Oh gosh!" I thought as I got out of bed to rescue the little rascal. I went to get a towel out of the bathroom to help shoo this little bat down off the picture frame and out the door; something I'd done with birds occasionally. I was balancing on a chair by the balcony doors, swatting the frame with a towel and trying my best to reach out and get this bat to come down. My then-husband was woken up by the commotion. "What are you doing?" he asked.

Half asleep I told him, "Well a bat flew in and around the bedroom and landed over here. I'm trying to help the poor little thing to fly back out." Dazed and sleepy I continued, "I don't know where it has gone. It was here, sitting on the wooden frame." At this point, I am convinced that its natural camouflage has blended it into the dark wood of the frame. Now I can't see it at all.

Then a sudden realization came to me. I blurted out, "Oh silly me, it was just Seeing-Eye Bat, my spirit guide!" Still half asleep, I was quite satisfied with my revelation, like it was a completely normal explanation. I promptly returned to bed.

The next morning my husband said to me, "Do you remember what you said last night?" I remembered every bit of it. Although, as I thought about what I had said, I admitted, "It's kind of weird, isn't it?"

Then it hit me. *Seeing-Eye Bat! But bats are blind!*–so they say. Only after I discovered my mediumship did it come to me. It was actually prophetic. Bats use their other senses to "see" more so than their physical eyes. A medium is someone who can see, not through their eyes but with their other senses.

I am now very grateful to have Seeing-Eye Bat as one of my animal spirit guides. He's there to help me with my other senses, my psychic senses, and to help with my connection to the other side. As I do my preparation for my healing work, readings, and especially animal communication, I check in with Seeing-Eye Bat and thank him.

Passed Over Animals

Animals that we had in our life and have now passed on are often around us as guides. They know us intimately and are our life partners. If you have a special connection with a pet, you can pretty much be assured that they will remain around you in spirit until they decide to reincarnate into your life again. You can connect and talk to these animals in spirit in exactly the same way you do with an animal who is living. They are listening and helping you, even if you are not consciously aware of it.

Animal Angels

You can call in angels to protect and heal your pets. When I first tried this, I was quite surprised who came to my aid.

Wally

I had a horse named Wally. Wally was more than just a horse for riding; he was my buddy, my pet. After many years of taking care of me, he retired to be a pet in my backyard. One day he wasn't feeling well. He stopped eating and had all the signs of colic. For those of you who have horses, you'll know that colic is when a horse is in gastrointestinal distress. Unlike people who can get over a stomachache pretty effortlessly, horses can easily die from colic.

As the vet came to treat Wally with oil to lubricate the digestive tract, I sent him Reiki healing. I then spent hours hoping and praying that he would pull through. It was in the early hours of the morning that I suddenly thought to call in the angels. *"Archangel Raphael, can you please send your strongest healing angels,"* I requested of Spirit.

Almost immediately, I saw a warm white glow forming toward Wally's rear. This light grew stronger and stronger until a large Pegasus angel appeared. I was completely surprised. I hadn't expected a horse angel. An angel in a human-like form would have better fit any expectations I may have had. That this was the form the angelic realm sent was even more confirmation to me that it really was otherworldly help that I was receiving and it was not my imagination.

My eyes swelled with gratitude as I was moved by this beautiful sight. Wally and I had indeed been sent an angel–a horse angel. I am not sure if the vet or anyone else saw it happen, but they were more than surprised at his rapid recovery.

CHAPTER 18

Power Animals

Native Americans believe we each have a Power Animal. This animal is assigned to us at birth, similarly to our spirit guide. Just as you communicate naturally with your pets, you are continually communicating with your Power Animal. They know you intimately. They are your partner and usually have an influence on your personality. People often take on the characteristics of their Power Animal. For instance, a person with a tiger as their Power Animal may come across as strong and powerful. This person may also have tiger print pillows or tiger artwork around their house. Perhaps they aren't even fully aware that they are collecting these items.

We can call on our Power Animal to assist and guide us whenever we do animal communication. Our Power Animal helps us to be more in touch with our instinctive animalistic side, allowing us to better understand and relate to the animal kingdom.

Your Power Animal is different from the pets you have loved and are now in spirit. It is usually different from your animal spirit guide. Some people find a stronger connection to their animal guide and others to their Power Animal. I believe they work in unison, and both influence and aid us in communication. The best way to meet your Power Animal is during a Native American journey to the underworld. Native Americans use the sound of drums to put themselves into a light trance as they meditate. Then they imagine going down into the earth on a spiritual journey. You call on your Power Animal to protect you on this journey.

You will know your Power Animal by the way they present themselves to you. They will show you three sides of themselves: their front, back, and side. We often take on the characteristics of our Power Animal. Try to guess the Power Animal of friends and family based on their personality. You will often be right. The following are a few examples of personality traits of the different Power Animals:

Alligator – They are quick-tempered, protective of their family, and will take revenge if they feel their family is threatened.

Ant – They are hard working. They work well in a team. They are determined, focused, and pay attention to the fine details.

Antelope – They are patient and loving but quick-witted and will move at a fast pace when they decide to do something.

Bear – They are the great protectors. They do well as the head of a large family or business. They have a lot of willpower and stamina to follow through.

Beaver – They are hardworking and great at building (either physical construction or a business project). They make wonderful homemakers.

Bird – They make great writers, actors, and others whose goal is to get the message out to others. They are creative with a flare for the dramatic.

Buffalo – They represent the traditional Native American protector. They are usually blessed with great abundance.

Bull – They never take "no" for an answer and can muscle their way into things, but you can count on them as a loyal friend.

Butterfly – They represent transformation and either go through transformation themselves or help others to transform.

Cat – They are independent thinkers. Very intelligent and even magical. They love their freedom and can be intolerant of others.

Crab – They are confident and very lucky in all they do and as a result, they are often extremely prosperous.

Dog – They are loyal, making strong long-term friendships. They are loving and family orientated.

Deer – They are usually quiet and cautious. They are graceful, gentle, and sweet. They carefully plan before making a move but will act quickly when the time is right.

Dragon – They are powerful, majestic, and great in business. They can also be fiery and short-tempered.

Elephant – They are very trustworthy, making long-term reliable friendships. They are wise and strong. They can be slow to move but always get the job done.

Fox – They are very intelligent and careful planners. They are able to change roles quickly and adapt to whatever situation they find themselves in.

Frog – They are easygoing and can sometimes be taken advantage of. They are very lucky with money.

Horse – They are family orientated. They love adventure but will always come back home to the herd. They are faithful and have stamina and endurance.

Lion – They like to be in the spotlight. Others love to be around them. They make great leaders. They possess great strength and courage.

Monkey – They love change. They are great comedians and entertainers and can be a bit of a trickster.

Mouse – They have a great eye for detail. They are careful planners. They are quick-witted and able to quickly resolve problems.

Owl – They are very wise. They like to observe before they act. They make great detectives and researchers. They often like to be awake at night.

Panther – They are careful planners but are ready to leap into action when the time comes. They are elegant and graceful.

Parrot – They make wonderful speakers, singers, and actors. They bring messages to the world.

Pig – They are often comedians. They are family orientated and love to give lots of affection. They are more intelligent than others give them credit for.

Rabbit – They tend to be shy. They like to be behind the scenes most of the time. They are great with children.

Swan – They are graceful, creative, and usually physically beautiful. They appreciate the finer things in life.

Snail – They are homebodies, preferring family time. They are loving, caring, and take pride in their home.

Snake – They are careful planners, innovative, and often medically inclined. They represent rebirth, transformation, and healing.

Unicorn – These are the mystics, psychics, and healers. It is hard to find them or get their attention but when you do, they will mesmerize you with their magical touch.

Tiger – They have strong personalities and are able to hold the attention of others. They display a lot of passion in all that they do. They come across as strong and powerful.

Tortoise – They are not usually quick to act, but very reliable and always get the job done. They can sometimes be a little shy.

Whale – They are very powerful and wise. They make strong leaders. They care about their families and put them before all else.

Wolf – They are family orientated. They are very intelligent and intuitive. They have a strong sense of honor and can be counted on to make the right decisions.

Zebra – They like to stand out in a crowd and make a difference in the world. They make great political leaders.

When you think of your Power Animal, what kind of traits would you normally associate with it? Do you have the same traits?

My First Journey

I was going through some life difficulties and had learned that you could contact your Native American Power Animal for help. I thought I'd try my hand at Native American journeying to the underworld to meet my Power Animal and find some answers. Shamans use a rhythmic drumbeat to put themselves into a trance-like state. As they listen to the sound of the drums and allow themselves to get into a deep meditational zone, they imagine going into the underworld (accompanied by their Power Animal).

However, all you really need is a relaxed mind and to allow your imagination to flow. I used a commercially purchased CD that was simply soft drumming for 30 minutes followed by a few minutes of faster drumming, a signal to head back home. This works very well in case you don't happen to have an intrepid friend to do the drumming for you.

I tuned into the sound of the drum and off I went on my journey. I imagined going down through a sacred hole leading to the center of the earth. The hole I'd chosen to visualize was strategically located behind a majestic waterfall. I had to climb up a large mountain and enter a cave behind the cascading falls to access the hole. It took me down a smooth slide, going deeper and deeper inside the mountain. It was there, deep in the mountain cave, that I met my Power Animal, a great beautiful falcon. "No, no, this is not right!" I declared. "My Power Animal is going to be a horse or tiger or something, not a bird. Not a falcon."

A thought quickly passed through my mind; my first company was called Falcon, an off-the-shelf name given by whoever was at the licensing office that day. I had also purchased one of those family crest plaque souvenirs for my mom a few years earlier. The name Thackray on an old English coat of arms happens to be represented by a falcon.

The bird said firmly, "Yes, I am your Power Animal." He then proceeded to show himself to me three ways: from the front, from the side, and from the back, which showed me that he was indeed my Power Animal.

"Now get on my wings, and I'll take you for a journey," he said. So I climbed aboard this majestic animal, and I was taken through the underworld. The underworld is not some dark place as the name might suggest. My underworld has a sky, beautiful meadows, lakes, waterfalls, and other tranquil settings. In fact, the underworld is a world just like our world with an above and below.

We were in the belly of the underworld when my Power Animal announced, "First, we are going to stop and pick up some medicine." Medicine. Hmm.... I thought maybe it would be something like sage, grains, herbs, or flowers, although I wasn't quite sure.

A cobra sprung out hissing from behind a rock. I jumped back in fright as my heart skipped a beat. I thought it was going to attack me. "Don't worry," said my falcon. "This is your medicine."

"Don't worry," confirmed the cobra. "I'm your friend. I will be your medicine." I'm not really sure about this, but okay. I accept that the cobra will be coming along with us on this journey.

We continued on our journey. In my quest I had specifically asked to find and remove any negative energy I may have been holding on to relating to a particular difficulty I was having. The falcon took me on a journey to meet some wise old men who gave me a message about my situation. I met other animals that gave me messages and advice as well. Although it felt like my imagination, the messages were so revealing and inspiring that I knew this guidance could not have been an invention of my own mind.

I heard the drumming getting quicker and quicker. It was now time to return to my earthly existence. I made my way back to the mountain, my heart pumping to the beat of the drums. Up through the mountain caverns I went until I was safely back at the waterfall. Here I said goodbye to my Power Animal. I know he's not too far away; that my falcon is always there, always around me. He is always protecting me and I can reach out to him whenever I need him.

It wasn't clear if this had been a dream, a feeling, or if it even existed in some kind of reality. However, if it was real in some other dimension, I had an indication that Native American protection was at play. Whether it was this journey that worked or it was something else, ultimately my difficult situation was resolved, and I had been blessed with spiritual guidance and protection.

CHAPTER 19

Alternative Healing

It is wonderful to see that many pet owners are now becoming aware of alternative healing for their pets and are more informed about their animal's nutrition. Chiropractic care, homeopathy, acupuncture, magnet therapy, and nutritionists for animals are becoming more widely offered than ever before.

Animals and Energy Healing

Animals are very sensitive to energy and they love to receive energy healing such as Reiki, crystal healing, Theta healing, sound therapy, light healing, and other modalities. They don't have the same blocks of disbelief that we sometimes have, as they understand that we are all energy beings. When I do Reiki on people, I find my cats and my dogs snoozing under my Reiki table. During my Reiki workshops, my dogs are constantly trying to get in on the energy.

Reiki for Animals

Reiki is an ancient form of energy healing rediscovered and put into a formal system by Mikao Usui in Japan in 1922. It involves placing the hands on or above the recipient and directing Reiki energy from guides in spirit. To do traditional Reiki, you need to be attuned to the energy by a Reiki Master. However, we are all giving and receiving this Reiki or Chi (life force) energy naturally, whether we are consciously aware of it or not. Do the palms of your hands sometimes get very hot or buzz after you place them on a person or an animal and try to send them healing energy? This is the Chi energy running through you. You are acting as a channel and the energy is being directed through you to the person or animal who is receiving the healing.

My Reiki Supervisor

I have a little Chihuahua. When I meditate in the morning, she sometimes jumps on my lap and nudges me to giver her Reiki. One morning she jumped on my lap and I asked, "Do you want Reiki?" This time I was very surprised by her response. "No, I want my Level I Reiki attunement!" she told me. So I gave her an attunement! She is now an official Reiki healer. Whenever I do attunements on my students, she comes running and sits down right next to us to supervise.

How to Give Energy Healing to an Animal

It is great to be trained in a specific healing modality to work on your pets. However, you do not need to be in order to simply send them some healing energy. First ask for protection and visualize a bubble of white light energy around you. Then rub your palms together, asking for healing energy to flow. Do this until you feel a buzzing or tingling sensation in your hands or heat from your palms. Be in your quiet place and ask your animal for permission to do energy healing on them. Ask your animal guides or any spirits and angels who wish to help for healing energy to flow to your pet. Then place your hands on or over the animal. Feel the energy. Start at their head and hold your hands over various areas for a minute or so, continuing down their body.

You may stroke your animal gently or hold your hands in a stationary position just on or above their head as you visualize healing energy flowing to them. Use your intuition to tune in and ask if you should keep your hands in one position longer or to move on. When your palms feel hotter or tingle more, that is a sign that the energy is flowing well and is needed in that area. You should hold this position longer.

Your animal will usually tell you when they have received enough energy by simply getting up and walking away. If you are not sure, about five minutes is fine. End by thanking your spiritual helpers and ask that they continue to work on your animal, if it is needed, even after you have finished the session.

Animal Chakras

Animals have the same chakras that we do, but actually their chakras stay clear and balanced far more easily than ours. However, as an animal gets older or health issues affect them, their chakras may become cloudy, off-balance, or blocked. You can check your pet's chakras using a pendulum.

A pendulum is basically any weight on the end of a string or chain. The ones that you can buy are usually made with a crystal, gemstone, or bit of metal. However, any pendant or handmade pendulum works equally well. Hold the string of your pendulum loosely between your thumb and forefinger. Don't move your pendulum deliberately, but allow it to make little movements. Now hold the pendulum over your pet's chakra and see if it rotates nice and smoothly. The pendulum actually follows the rotation of the chakra in a similar way to how a magnet works. This enables you to see if the energy of the chakra is flowing well. The pendulum should show a smooth and consistent rotation in either direction. If it seems slow or sticky, go ahead and direct some healing energy as I described above and then retest with the pendulum.

You can use the pendulum to ask yes/no questions about your pet's health as well. To do this, ask your pendulum to show you what a "yes" answer looks like. Watch which way it rotates. Then ask your pendulum to show you a "no" answer. Watch which way it rotates. Your "yes" may be your pendulum swinging backwards and forwards. Your "no" may be your pendulum rotating counterclockwise. This will be your yes/no indication from Spirit from now on. The motion for yes/no will be individual to each person. (See Appendix A for more detailed instructions on how to use a pendulum).

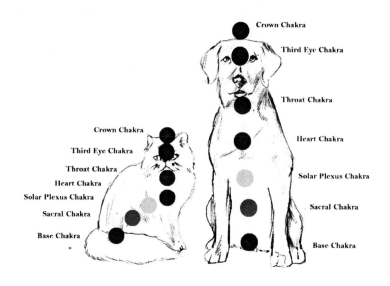

Spring Water

What I hear more often than not from people's animals is to please give them "fresh clean drinking water." I find they prefer "spring water" to regular purified water. What I see is that with love and clean water, our pets can flush out a lot of negative energy.

Crystals and Gemstones

There are many different colors and types of crystals, and each have different healing properties. In general, animals react very well to crystal healing as they are very sensitive to the energies. Put a crystal in your pet's bed, in their water dish, or by their food. You can even attach a crystal pet charm to their collar. Just be sure it is safe not to tangle or get caught. (I have a line of crystal charms with specific healing properties that can be hung on their collar.)

Remember to cleanse your crystals every month. You can cleanse them by placing them under running water, leaving them overnight in salt water, or burning sage and letting the smoke flow over them. Quartz crystals will help to clear your environment of negative energies as well as clear and enhance the positive energy in the room.

The following are a few of the crystals and gemstones that I find particularly useful, especially for certain issues. I have categorized them by their properties.

For universal (general) healing: *Clear quartz*
Clear quartz crystals are the universal healing stone and are wonderful healing tools for animals.

For increased connection:
Turquoise, Larimar, or any turquoise-colored stone
Larimar is known as the "communication stone" and also the "dolphin stone." It is wonderful for aiding animal communication. Other turquoise stones also work well. Turquoise is the color of the Throat Chakra, which represents communication. Place this stone on your animal's collar and also around your own neck to aid your communication.

To reduce anxiety: *Rose quartz or moonstone*
My favorite stone to reduce anxiety is the rose quartz. This beautiful pink stone represents love. If you have an animal who gets anxious when you leave, try placing a piece of rose quartz by their bed or place a small charm on their collar. If you also get anxious about them getting anxious, try this yourself.

To increase strength and vitality:
Red, orange, or black stones. Hematite or heliotrope (bloodstone)
For an animal who is old, weak, or needs strength, try a small charm on their collar of hematite (dark grey) or bloodstone (deep red). You may also want to place these stones around their food and water bowls.

For psychic connection or to connect with Spirit:

Amethyst or lapis lazuli

To enhance your Third Eye, you may wear these stones. If you believe your animal has a past life connection as a healer or mystical animal, using these stones around them will aid their connection. Lapis lazuli is a spiritual stone that was used in ancient Egypt and is especially good for great healing cats. You may also wear these stones when you ask to connect with your pets in spirit.

To remove negative energy from your environment:

Smoky quartz

Place a piece of smoky quartz in your home, next to their food bowl, or in a place where you feel there is negative energy. It will absorb negative energies in your pet's environment.

If you prefer, you can always use a clear quartz crystal. Clear quartz crystals can be programmed to aid with any healing or for protection. Just say a prayer over your crystal, placing the intention into it.

CHAPTER 20

Exotic Pets & Wild Animals

How to Communicate with a Wild Animal

Although you can communicate with wild animals, they are not used to this type of interaction. Dogs, cats, horses, and other domesticated animals are used to us constantly talking to them (whether we realize it or not). Not only are we verbally talking to them, but they are also receiving our thought packages almost non-stop when we are around them. So when we make a conscious effort to communicate with them, it is not really anything new.

When we communicate with a wild animal, it is a huge surprise. "What, are you talking to me?!" Might be the response. You may also find them busily engaged in their own life and reluctant to engage. The first time I spoke with a squirrel, she let me know that she had lots of work to do. She talked to me but didn't slow for a moment as she was actively collecting acorns. She never took a break as she spoke, like we would do, but rather continued preparing her stash for her youngsters. This is often the case in the wild. Their life depends on collecting food and other necessary routines and so talking with you is secondary.

Of course when you are communicating, you are communicating with the animal's higher self, so what they are doing at the time doesn't really matter. What you do pick up on, though, is their earthly personality, their attitude, and their likes and dislikes. The personality, goals, and the thoughts that occupy their mind are usually very different from a domesticated animal.

Exotic pets may have been raised in the wild, captured, and turned into pets. In this case they still have a wild streak and may not talk to you as much or as easily as an exotic pet raised in captivity.

Attracting Wild Animals

Some people may attract wild animals. For instance, birds and squirrels may like to always be in their yard. Perhaps they often notice coyotes wandering or hawks flying overhead. This likely has something to do with your animal guides and a connection you have with that species. If you have been chosen by that species, it is a wonderful blessing and you can ask them questions.

Reptiles

You can also communicate with snakes, turtles, lizards, and the like. However, I believe that certain people have a better connection with reptiles than others and you have a better chance of communicating if you resonate with them. If you are afraid of snakes, they will pick up on that and it will make it more difficult for you to have a good connection. Try your best to put yourself into the body of the animal and become that animal. If you succeed at this, you will overcome any trepidation that you may have.

You may presume that there isn't much range in personality in the reptile world. For example, you may assume that all tortoises act the same. Actually they are all very individual and can have a wide range of personality traits, just like any other animal.

A Day at the Zoo

The next time you go to the zoo, try being in the communication zone and you may see the animals from a whole new perspective.

In my experience, animals at the zoo seem to fall into three categories: those who feel saved from a dangerous and difficult environment and they prefer their new life; those who miss their native environment and long to be back in the wild even if it was not the easiest life; and those who were raised in captivity, and therefore, do not really have an understanding of what it is like in the wild. Although, I feel that this last group does have some sense of what it would be like in the wild. (Remember they can experience through others elsewhere, as did the monkeys of the hundredth monkey theory. They had knowledge of an experience without having had the actual experience first.)

These animals raised in captivity often do not wish to be in the wild because they haven't learned the skills to be able to cope on their own in the wild and may be fearful that they wouldn't survive. There is really a fourth category, as well, of those who feel that they have a mission to teach people and to represent their species. These selfless creatures are more concerned with their important role of helping to bring a message to the world, rather than their own personal desires.

Zoos also offer a good opportunity to test your skills. It is interesting to first talk to the animal and then read the informational plaque displayed to see how accurate you were. I wouldn't tell the zookeepers you were given any messages from the animals, though, as you may be politely escorted out. You can also take notes and confirm any details you received about the species later online.

There may be the occasional animal at the zoo who is not interested in talking to you. However, many animals there tend to be a bit bored and welcome a little telepathic chat time.

Ants, Spiders, and Other Insects

Yes, you can even talk to ants, spiders, and other insects. Ants work very much as a team so when you talk to them, you are likely to be answered by the whole group at once. Ants normally have a purpose and are determined to carry on with their task so it is difficult to get their attention. We could learn a lot about teambuilding and working in unison from ants. As you see them work, it is clear that they are always communicating and in sync with one another.

For me, I cannot have a meaningful conversation with an ant in the same way that I can with a cat, for instance. Perhaps it's just me because I don't relate to them or find them as interesting as a cat but perhaps some people do. Normally I only talk to ants when they are tracking through my kitchen. In our communication I have found that they are usually looking for water. Then it's an easy bribe to place a small container of water where you would like them to go.

As far as spiders, I don't like to kill them. So unless it's a black widow or another dangerous type, I try to catch them and free them outside. Talking to them gently helps me to catch them more easily.

Dolphins

Dolphins are thought to have been present in Lemurian and Atlantean times and have long been recognized for their magical qualities. More recently, New Age thinkers have come to understand that dolphins have an important role on this planet. Even if they are not sure what the dolphin purpose is, they know this role is a bigger one than we can see on the surface.

Researchers have taken note of dolphins and their ability to be trained. Some have even found that when dolphins are shown visual images telepathically, the dolphin has been able to carry out these visual "instructions." It makes you wonder who is doing the training here? They must look at these researchers as fledgling beings just developing their intuition. I am sure the dolphins feel that we are the ones in school being taught by them and not the other way around.

The first time I swam with wild dolphins what impressed me right away was that they did not appear to be separate beings. Yes, they had individuality, yet they also seemed to work as a collective consciousness. As I tuned in to talk to one, it was as if a whole collective spoke back. I watched as they gently slid back and forth, diving and rolling over, as if to play with me. Much of the time they swam in unison. As one made a sharp turn, diving down and then up, all of them simultaneously joined in. It didn't seem that there was a leader. Somehow they were all tuned in, making collective decisions totally in sync. One or two would break off and do their own thing for a minute and then return, perfectly and smoothly, to join in the latest stroke of the collective.

As I sank into my being and communicated from a place of love, an overwhelming sense of peace and tranquility came over me. This love that was coming back was not from only one dolphin with whom I was communicating, but rather a whole collective consciousness.

Rather than ask questions about their likes and dislikes, I felt I had an audience of wise sages, ready to advise me. I felt their reasoning was so far in advance of mine and that they had such a close connection to Divine Source that it was like being in Divine presence itself.

As I asked questions pertaining to my life, nothing seemed quite so complicated anymore. All of the answers came from my own thoughts but were more directed. It was as if I was gently nudged to bring forth my own advice for my own lessons. I describe it as similar to a therapist who would gently guide you to make your own conclusion, rather than simply telling you an answer. I was being gently guided through my own thoughts and all the answers that came were surprisingly simple, wise, and contained a sense of peace and tranquility. I found swimming with the dolphins to be enlightening and beautiful.

Dangerous Animals

Be careful when communicating with an animal that might be dangerous to you. Just because you feel like you are communicating well doesn't mean to say that you should get dangerously close to them. Remember, they still have powerful instincts that take precedence over any nice communication session you may be having if they feel threatened or frightened.

Hummingbirds and Butterflies

I often hear people say that they see butterflies as a reminder of passed over loved ones. For instance, they may see a white butterfly that appears every time they think of their father who is now in spirit. I've also heard many reports of unusual displays of butterflies at funerals. I believe this is because people in spirit are able to manifest butterflies very easily. So it is not that their father has become a butterfly, but rather it is because their father in spirit is able to send a butterfly as a sign to his loved one that he is around. Our animals in spirit can also send butterflies to give us a sign.

Butterflies are also a symbol of transformation. Just as a butterfly has transformed from a caterpillar into this beautiful form, we too transform from the physical body into spirit.

To me, just as butterflies are sent from spirits, hummingbirds are sent from angels. I often see hummingbirds when I meditate. I see them when I feel closely protected by Divine Source and especially when I ask for a connection to the angels. That being said, I do live in California. Perhaps it would be easier for angels to send a little sparrow or other type of bird in other parts of the world.

Butterflies are sent from spirits. Hummingbirds are sent from angels.

To communicate with wild animals, insects, or exotic animals:

- Use caution if they are dangerous. Don't expect that being in communication with them will prevent danger.

- Connect in the same way as with a domesticated animal.

- It may take a little more to connect, as they are not as used to this type of interaction.

- Respect their time if they appear busy.

- You may find that you have a special connection with a specific kind of wild animal.

CHAPTER 21

Animal Communication Workshop

I have developed and teach animal communication workshops that I mostly hold at my ranch in California. In teaching I've found that the most difficult hurdle is not "how to communicate," but rather how to remove the blocks that we have created in ourselves. These blocks give us the false notion that animal communication is simply not possible or that we cannot trust and believe that we can communicate in this way. In my workshops we initially spend time on exercises to get the creative juices flowing without the pressure of trying to communicate.

I think it is useful, even though you are not with me in a workshop, to run through the exercises in your mind so that you can see the flow. After all, it has been scientifically shown that imagining you are doing something, such as being present and participating in a workshop, can produce the same results (as long as what you are imagining is vivid and strong enough). You can also use this framework to create your own workshop or to practice developing this skill with your friends. The following is a typical workshop.

Animal Communication Weekend Workshop Schedule

How Animal Communication Works

I open my workshops by discussing how animal communication works and what it feels like. I emphasize that one of the most difficult aspects is to distinguish between what is your imagination and what is real communication. Almost everyone wonders, "Is this all in my mind? Am I making this up?" I explain how important it is to know that animal communication comes through our thoughts and from the same place as our imagination. We start by allowing ourselves to "make things up" so that our creative thought process can flow.

Meet Your Animal Spirit Guide

I lead a guided meditation to meet your animal guide (See Chapter Four). Then we discuss what everyone experienced. People are often very surprised by how their personality reflects the characteristics of their animal guide. Sometimes a passed over pet comes through as well.

Exercises

Partner up and practice the exercises described in Chapter Five. This allows you to become more comfortable with using your imagination and removes some of the intellectual blocks that prevent us from believing. People are often astounded by how well they do in these exercises.

Practice with Photos

Each student shares photos of their animals, alive or in spirit (it doesn't matter and we don't say upfront). Again everyone partners up to do practice readings using photos of animals they don't know.

I guide everyone through the steps: protect, get in the communicating zone, ask permission, send and receive love, etc. Then I ask the partner communicating to visualize the animal's food bowl. If at first it doesn't come, fill the bowl using their imagination.

Try to envision yourself in the animal's body and what it really feels like to be them. Now imagine a toy or activity that the animal likes to play. Imagine this from the animal's point of view. Then ask the animal to take you on a tour of their home. Note specific details: what the outside looks like, the floor, windows, a favorite chair, where they sleep, etc. At the end of the exercise each person shares the information that they saw during the exercise with their partner and discusses what insights he or she had.

Most students will have picked up on something. However, I find that many times they simply don't trust it and will say something like, "I was going to say that" or "I got that, but I didn't say it because I didn't think it meant anything." I encourage my students to say everything they picked up on, even if it seemed strange or insignificant. It might be that amazing little gem we are looking for. We do several exchanges of photos.

Automatic Writing

Instead of the one-on-one sessions described above, the whole group is going to be tuning in together to a single animal. I use a photo of one of my pets with whom we will communicate. I guide the class through the communication steps (protect, get in the communicating zone, ask permission, send and receive love, etc) and then ask questions to the group as a whole.

My students then do automatic writing. Basically they are instructed to jot things down as they pop into their head. Some may feel themselves writing whole sentences and others only a word or phrase. The questions I ask are things like:

- 🐾 What is your favorite food?
- 🐾 What is your favorite activity?
- 🐾 Describe where you sleep.

- ❧ What do you enjoy doing?
- ❧ Who are your animal friends?
- ❧ What ails you?
- ❧ What major life events have happened to you?
- ❧ What quirks do you have?

I pick an animal who has had several interesting life events. It's amazing how many students are accurate in their description and even identify key aspects of the life event.

Describing an Animal

Each student is given a photograph and will get up, one at a time, in front of the group to describe the animal. They begin by following the steps to connect. First they are to simply describe what they visually see in the actual photo (nothing psychic yet). This helps the student to get used to describing without forcing. They are then directed to continue, but now to allow their imagination to start describing things that cannot be seen in the photograph. This would be things like the animal's personality, history, likes and dislikes, what is going on in their life right now, their health, etc. At the end, the student who brought the photograph will let us know what was accurate.

In Person Animals

After the group has practiced on several photos, we move on to live animals. (Normally this happens the second day of the workshop.) I start with one of my dogs and tell everyone what questions to ask him/her. Each person tunes in at the same time. I have found my dogs have no problem responding to everyone's questions at once. At the end we share our experiences. Students usually find that although the process is similar to using a photograph, having the animal present can be distracting and therefore a little more difficult.

Health

I discuss areas of health, including:

* How to ask animals about their health issues
* Possible causes of health issues
* Checking the animal's environment
* How to do a body scan
* Animal Reiki
* Chakras and auras
* Using pendulums and dowsing for health questions
* How animals mimic their owner's health or energy
* Natural healing

In Person Health Subject

I use a live animal to practice identifying health issues. I usually choose one of my dogs who is a real ham and is quite happy to sit at the front of the class being the center of attention. A couple of my dogs have interesting health histories. The group tunes in, asks some light chitchat questions, and then we are ready to begin. I instruct the group what questions to ask their subject about health. The students will often pick up ailments at this initial stage, but I tell them to keep their insights until the end.

I then lead the group through a body scan. We psychically scan each part of the animal's body from their head down to their toes. The students are directed at each area to tune in to their own body and use it as a gauge. Do they feel something in their own body that is an indication of an issue in the same area on the animal?

Each student then takes a turn stroking the dog to feel its energy. This gives the students a last chance to see if what they detected psychically in the body scan feels the same when they physically touch the energy of the animal. At the end we share what insights the group got regarding their subject's health. Usually there are similar findings within the group.

Passed Over Animals

I share my experiences of talking to animals in spirit and what they have expressed to me about their passing and the spirit world they live in. Topics include:

- ❧ Transition and the process of passing over for animals
- ❧ Pets in spirit around us
- ❧ Reincarnation and past lives
- ❧ How to tell if an animal is living or has passed on
- ❧ I then lead a meditation to connect with our pets who are now in spirit

Angels

Our angels are here to help us. I talk about angels and calling upon an animal's angels and guardians for healing and protection. If we have a photo of an ill animal in need of healing, we do a group healing session for them. We call in the angels for this animal and ask for them to assist in our session.

Communication to Modify Behaviors and Reassure

What might be causing poor behavior or a bad habit? I explore common problems such as peeing and pooping in the house, barking, anxiety, chewing furniture, etc. We use specific issues of animals whose photos we have in the group. I usually do a sample reading of the animal as well.

We discuss how to handle moving, being away from your pets, nervous animals, and "pet peeves." We also discuss giving an animal a role in the family and figuring out their "job." We may do another group reading, as well, on someone's pet.

Talk to the Horses

I happen to live on a ranch with happy horse volunteers available. Students gather around the subjects as a group and tune in. I direct questions for them to ask the horses. What are their names? Favorite food? Are any of them related and in what way?

What do they like to do? What are they afraid of? I also direct the students to ask questions about specific things the horses may know about, such as events that happened on the ranch recently.

Talk to Other Kinds of Animals

I usually bring my turtle, chickens, snake, or some other less common pet so that my students can have a go at talking with animals they may not be as familiar with. Then we walk around the ranch where we can usually find a good selection of birds, squirrels, and other wild creatures to practice on.

Tracking a Lost Pet

Often there will be a student who brings a photo of a lost pet. If this is the case, we will attempt do a "lost animal reading" together. I also tune in and direct the students in the questions I am asking. At the end we see what information we collectively got. Hopefully after class the owner will have a successful reunion story to share with the group.

Your Pet As Your Partner

We discuss what role your pets have in your life. Perhaps you have a healing animal. We partner up to read each other's photos and often get information about the animal's role with their owner.

I also use one of my dogs as a soothsayer. The students telepathically ask my dog a question about their own life and see if they get a message. Another method is for the student to pull a Tarot card to reveal the answer to their question. (The animal is directing us in which card to choose.) A profound answer is often found.

Practice Photos

The following are photos to use for practice sessions and to develop your animal communication skills. Below each photo is a list of sample questions to ask during your session. You are not limited to these questions, they are just a guide to help get you started. On the next page you will find a description and history of the animal. Try not to peek at this before you do the session. Remember, once you look at the description, you'll know all about them. Make your session really count before you look.

Be sure to be ready and focused for each session. Follow the steps I've outlined and get as much information from your communication session as you can. During the session, try to put yourself inside their body. You may do a body scan for health if you feel you need it. You may even use your pendulum over the photo.

After the session, compare what you got to the animal's description on the back of the photo. If you picked up on something that isn't listed, it could be something that the animal gave you. However, you will only have the facts in the description to verify.

Animal 1 Questions

1. What is my favorite food?

2. Where do I live?

3. Where do I sleep? Show me by remote viewing.

4. Who are my animal friends?

5. Do I have any unusual features?

6. How did I come to the family (was I purchased or rescued)?

7. Am I here or in spirit?

8. How is my health? If I have passed, how was my health and how did I pass?

9. How do I feel physically?

10. What is my job or role in the family?

11. Did you get a sense of my personality?

12. Did you get my name?

Animal 1 Description

My name is Nala, like in the film *The Lion King*. I'm a girl. Gail is my mom.

I live on a ranch with horses, so I spend most of the time outdoors. I love splashing in our stream.

I like all food. I may tell you about how I like to pick up the dog bowl (even though it is really heavy) and carry it around the yard, spilling half the food. I guard my food from the other dogs. I love to eat the clippings from the horse's hooves.

I like to sleep outside most of the time on my mom's sun lounges that are striped.

I have one brown eye and one blue eye. I am always told how pretty my eyes are.

We have a family of several dogs. Max is my friend. He's a black lab mix. But my dearest friend in the world was Bob, a large tan lab mix, who is now in spirit. He's the one mom tells the story about where he came back for a short while. I had a brother who also had different-colored eyes, but he was a darker brown. We were separated at about a year old.

I arrived at the family as a puppy, only a few weeks old. My brother and I were found by a lady postman who begged Gail's mom to take us. We were in a terrible state and covered in ticks. I am definitely the matriarch of the family.

I am about 15 years old now and although I have a few lumps and cysts, nothing bothers me.

Animal 2 Questions

1. What is my favorite food?

2. Where do I live?

3. Where do I sleep? Show me by remote viewing.

4. Who are my animal friends?

5. How did I come to the family (was I purchased or rescued)?

6. Who do I belong to?

7. Am I here or in spirit?

8. How is my health? If I have passed, how was my health and how did I pass?

9. How do I feel physically?

10. Did you get a sense of my personality?

11. What is my job or role in the family?

12. Is there an unusual talent that I have?

13. Did you get my name?

Animal 2 Description

My name is Akai, a little like the Acai berry but spelled differently. I'm a girl. My name before was Tina.

I live with my mom, Gail. I am allowed to go in and out of the house. I play in the stream, but only when my mom is with me.

I love tidbits of people food. My dried dog food, not so much. Sometimes I get little chewy bones. I like to sleep on mom's bed. Sometimes I get caught going inside mom's bed and under the covers. The cover is green. There is also a burgundy dog bed I sleep in during the day.

We have a family of several dogs. My first best friends were two other small dogs named Leo and Sweet Pea, but they passed away.

I was purchased as a pup for Rachel's 15th Birthday. The place where I was bred was a pony farm. When Rachel went to college, Gail became my mom.

I am quite shy and get a little scared sometimes, but I am very sweet. When I get to know you, I am very loving.

My mom does Reiki and I asked my mom for my Reiki Level I attunement. So mom attuned me as a healer. I love to be around when mom teaches Reiki, and I am a healing dog.

I had a little surgery on my neck. It was hard and swollen, and the vet thought the abscess was caused by a thorn. I told my mom it was an insect that I ate, something like a scorpion.

I am about five years old and in good health.

Animal 3 Questions

1.   What is my favorite toy?

2.   How did I come to the family (was I purchased or rescued)?

3.   Did I have a previous owner?

4.   Where do I live?

5.   Are there other animals around me?

6.   Where do I sleep?

7.   Am I here or in spirit?

8.   How is my health? If I have passed, how was my health and how did I pass?

9.   Did you get a sense of my personality?

10. Are there some things that irritate me?

11. What is my job or role in the family?

12. What do I think about children?

13. Did you get my name?

Animal 3 Description

My name is Kiwi. I'm an Abyssinian. I'm a girl.

My favorite toy is a mouse with a rattle. When I was younger, I used to play fetch. My mommy Buffi got me from her friend Scott when I was two. Scott bought me at the pet store. He also had another cat and dog. Scott used to travel a lot and would leave me. That's why he gave me to my new mommy and daddy.

It was hard at first because they had four other cats. I was even on antidepressants for a while because the other cats bullied me. I feel better about them now and learned to fight back when I got bullied. But still I prefer humans. Mommy and daddy also have dogs, but I'm not friendly with them. I am the "protector" of the upstairs and if the dogs get past the gate, I chase them away, hissing and swatting.

My favorite place to sleep during the day is in a denim chair or on the bed. I stretch and roll over when mommy changes the sheets. Each night I sit on mommy's shoulder for cuddle time, and I purr and drool. I like my "kitty cave time" where I go under the covers to escape the other cats at night. I am first in line for a morning cuddle when I wake up.

As I have gotten older, I don't like other people as much. I just like my mommy and daddy. I've become wary of children (I told Gail this was because of the pet shop experience), but I'll put up with them petting me.

I am healthy and very much alive.

Animal 4 Questions

1.   Where did I come from? (Hint – It's another country.)

2.   Have I had more than one owner?

3.   Where do I live?

4.   What breed am I?

5.   What is my job?

6.   What am I like with other animals?

7.   Do I take care of other animals?

8.   What do I dislike or am afraid of?

9.   Am I here or in spirit?

10.   How old am I?

11.   How is my health? If I have passed, how was my health and how did I pass?

12.   Did you get a sense of my personality?

13.   Did you get my name?

Animal 4 Description

My name is Audrey de la Tour. I just go by Audrey.

I was born in France and even have a passport. My old owner (a man) later shipped me to Mexico where I lived for about a year and then I came to California. My mom, Gail kept me at different stables in L.A. and then I moved to Gail's ranch. I am a show jumper and very good at it. I jump big jumps and I'm fast. I get scared sometimes, but I have perfect form and a lot of talent. I know I can be difficult to ride.

I am an Anglo-Arab and have an "AA" tattoo. This means I am part Thoroughbred and part Arab, but I look like a Thoroughbred.

I am not very tolerant of other animals. When Gail's dogs come into my pen, I put my ears back and chase them. I have been known to nip and kick other horses. People occasionally get a nip too!

I've been a mom three times. Once in France, and Gail bred me twice (I had a boy and a girl).

I am afraid of water. I told Gail it was from my owner in Mexico who made me skid in a big puddle. I don't like doing water jumps, and I argued with Gail about it.

I am in spirit now. I lived to be an old lady in my twenties and retired on Gail's ranch. I was playing in my pen, chasing dogs, and I slipped and broke my leg. I am now very happy running around in a pasture in heaven.

Animal 5 Questions

1. Where do I live?

2. Who is my owner?

3. What is my favorite food?

4. What is my favorite thing to do?

5. Where do I sleep? Show me by remote viewing.

6. Who are my animal friends?

7. How did I come to the family (was I purchased or rescued)?

8. What is my job or role in the family?

9. Am I here or in spirit?

10. How is my health? If I have passed, how was my health and how did I pass?

11. How do I feel physically?

12. Did you get a sense of my personality?

13. Did you get my name?

Animal 5 Description

My name is Leo. I'm a Miniature Dachshund. I live at the ranch with my mom Gail. My best friend is Akai. She's a little Chihuahua, but I like all the big dogs, too.

My dad bought me as a tiny pup. When my dad moved away, my mom adopted me. I also have two human sisters. My role in the family is definitely to love everyone.

I love to eat. That's a bit of a problem because I tend to get fat. Mom tries to keep me on dried dog food, but I love treats. I especially love the clippings off the horse's hooves when they get shod. My favorite thing to do is to chase lizards. I'd like to eat them, but my mom usually rescues them.

I love to go to the beach and go for walks on the boardwalk. Sometimes I used to lie under the stroller when my human sisters were babies. I sleep in a soft burgundy bed that is kept under the coffee table, so it has sort of a roof.

I've had pretty major health issues. When I was about nine, I had a slipped disc in my back. My legs were completely paralyzed, which really hurt, and I couldn't walk to go pee and poop. My mom took me for a very expensive surgery where they removed the disc completely. After about 6 months of intensive care and recovery, I was back to almost 100%.

Other health issues bothered me. When I was still with my dad as a pup, I got attacked by a big dog and had a broken leg and other injuries. I also get skin issues.

I finally passed when I was about twelve years old. That was a pretty good age for a Dachshund. I just got really old and my kidneys finally gave out.

Animal 6 Questions

1. What is my favorite food?
2. Where do I live?
3. How did I come to the family (was I purchased or rescued)?
4. Do I have a role in the family?
5. What do I like?
6. Am I here or in spirit?
7. How is my health? If I have passed, how was my health and how did I pass?
8. How do I feel physically?
9. Did you get a sense of my personality?
10. Did you get my name?

Animal 6 Description

My name is Katrina, like hurricane Katrina, but I got named just before it actually happened. My then ten-year-old mom named me. My mom guessed I was a girl and she was correct.

I live on turtle food, but a couple of times I got fish and they were yummy! They weren't really meant as my dinner though.

I came from a street vendor. I originally came from Mexico and it felt like some kind of breeding farm rather than from the wild. I was very small, about the size of a quarter when I arrived, but I've grown a lot. My mom was a little girl who was really good with me. Eventually she grew up and I was passed down to another little girl.

My role in the family is to teach the youngsters responsibility for having a pet. I'm pretty easy to take care of, so I'm a good first pet. The girls sometimes clean and polish my belly shell that makes me feel great.

I'm still alive and well. I've never had any real health problems, and I'm about seven years old.

I'm pretty easygoing. Sometimes I get a little scared and keep my head inside my shell if I feel threatened. I did bite someone once, but it was a visitor who put her finger right into my mouth.

Animal 7 Questions

1. Where do I live?

2. Where do I sleep? Show me by remote viewing.

3. Who are my animal friends?

4. How did I come to the family (was I purchased or rescued)?

5. Who do I belong to?

6. Do I have any bad habits?

7. Am I here or in spirit?

8. How is my health? If I have passed, how was my health and how did I pass?

9. How do I feel physically?

10. Did you get a sense of my personality?

11. What is my job or role in the family?

12. Did you get my name?

Animal 7 Description

My name is Hank. I live at the ranch with Gail. I was adopted from the pound by Gail's friend Lilly. She couldn't keep me, so Gail agreed to adopt me. I was about one at the time. I get to run around the ranch during the day and then at night I like to sleep on the couch. It's a burgundy color.

My friends are Max and Nala. They are in charge. I am the youngster of the group. I used to be a little bit afraid of Max, but he's not so bad.

I love to chase the neighbor's car. My mom gets upset with me and always talks to me about it. I am good when she is there, but if I think she can't see me, I can't help myself.

I had a strange health issue. My right leg swelled up like a balloon. I told my mom I got bit on my paw by a rattlesnake or scorpion. I was sniffing in the long grass when it happened. It took a few weeks to heal. Another time I got bit by something on my left cheek and it swelled up, too.

I'm fun and everybody loves me. I'm the greeter. I like to put my front feet up on people's laps if they let me. I try to climb on my mom's lap or in bed with her, but she says I'm too big.

I once wandered just outside my gate. I was "rescued" by a well-meaning person and taken a long way from home. My mom got me back.

I'm about four years old, alive, happy, and healthy.

Animal 8 Questions

1. How did I come to the family?

2. Where do I live?

3. Where do I sleep?

4. Who are my animal friends?

5. Who do I belong to?

6. Am I here or in spirit?

7. How is my health? If I have passed, how was my health and how did I pass?

8. How do I feel physically?

9. Did you get a sense of my personality?

10. What is my job or role in the family?

11. Did you get my name?

Animal 8 Description

My name is Banky. I was born in April 2000 in Illinois. My mom Danielle adopted me and my brother Maynard at six weeks old. We drove cross-country to Los Angeles. I was allowed to sleep on mom's lap while she was driving.

I like to think I'm sweet, curious, and a super social kitty who loves his mom, most people, and my brother. Sometimes my mom's friends, family, and boyfriends help take care of me.

When we were kittens, we were playing and knocked over a big box. It landed on me and I broke my hip! I rebounded quickly after surgery. I then had urinary crystals in 2008.

In 2012, my rear left leg went lame. For a few days I was unable to walk, but now I can walk, jump, and play! I still walk stiffly with a bit of a limp, and I occasionally lose balance or my toes knuckle under. But, overall, I'm so much better! It's a mystery what happened, but I told Gail it had to do with a pinched nerve in my spine.

I love to sit near my chosen people and get TONS of love. I like to observe, but sometimes I want to be in the middle of everything – especially if it involves exploring your bag! I'm always the first one to greet people and animals who come over.

I love Greenie treats and have a love/hate relationship with my fabric Cat Charmer toy!

I am a total mama's boy, but I am pretty friendly with most people. I like to flash my belly at people to get attention. I must admit that I love the sound of my own voice!

I sleep on the bed if mom is not in. If mom is in bed, I like to sleep in a spot where I can see her and watch over her.

Spread the Word

It is my wish for you to commit to passing along this knowledge, to use it, and to educate others. I hope that in reading this book, you will have a new respect for the world we share with our animals and that you will do your part to make it the best place for all of us to live.

A Prayer to St. Francis of Assisi

For his love for all creatures.

St. Francis is the patron saint of animals.

We celebrate St. Francis on his feast day, October 4th, when ceremonies blessing the animals may be held.

You can call on St. Francis during your prayers and meditations to help you communicate more strongly. Ask St. Francis to help you when you are healing an animal, looking for a lost pet, or when your pet is in need. Call on St. Francis to help you talk to your animals and to guide you in helping animals everywhere.

A Prayer to St. Francis of Assisi

Dear Saint Francis, patron saint of all animals. You who loved animals during life and now in spirit are the protector of all God's creatures. From the fish in the sea to the birds in the sky, from those in spirit to those on Earth, you love all animals big and small. Help me to communicate with animals in the way you do. Help me to love and respect them in the way you do. Help me to heal them in the way you do and guide me in their loving care.

In particular, please watch over my pet _____ in spirit.

In particular, please send healing to my pet _____ for _____ .

In particular, please guide my pet _____ safely home.

Thank you Saint Francis for your never-ending love for animals. Please be around me and my animals, now and always. Amen.

Acknowledgments

I want to acknowledge those who dedicate their life to the alleviating the plight of animals. For you are the true angels of the world.

I would like to thank all those who shared stories of themselves and their pets.

And with deep appreciation, I would like to thank the following people:

My family: my mom and my girls, who believe in me and support me through my crazy adventures. My Auntie Pauline and Cousin Ric, my spiritual sounding boards.

My dear friend Mara, without whom this book would probably never have been published. And to Dawn of Teagarden Designs who helped her put this together. Thank you to Buffi and Danielle and their wonderful kitties, Kiwi and Banky. And Peter for guiding me. A special mention to my dear friend Mark, who has supported me from the beginning of my journey.

And especially to my spiritual group and friends who have attended, volunteered, and supported me at my events.

Appendix A
Pendulums

What Is a Pendulum?

Basically any weight on the end of a string or chain will act as a pendulum. You can also find beautiful ones made of gemstones, crystals, or metals (e.g., copper). The pendulum carries the energy of the material or particular crystal that it is made from. Pendulums come in different shapes. The most common is the traditional cone shape with a point at the end. Egyptian pendulums are more elongated and can have distinctive geometric forms. Other shapes may include round balls or star-shaped.

How to Use Your Pendulum

To use your pendulum, follow these simple instructions:

- ❧ Before you start always protect yourself with Divine white light as you would with any connection to Spirit.
- ❧ Ask if you have a spirit from the white light working through your pendulum. (Instructions on how to find your YES sign are below.)

Asking Yes/No Questions

❧ To begin, put your pendulum in the resting position. To do this, take a deep breath, relax your mind, clear your thoughts, and just allow the pendulum to stop (hanging straight down and still).

❧ You are now going to set definite directions for yes/no answers. These directions are unique to each person. Hold the pendulum chain between two fingers, allowing the pendulum to hang freely. Say, "Give me a 'Yes.'" Your pendulum will start to swing. Either it will swing back and forth, or side to side, or it will rotate in a circle either clockwise or counterclockwise. This direction you have established is now your "Yes" answer. This will be "Yes" for any pendulum you use. Now use the same method to find your "No."

❧ When you ask a question, your pendulum will move in the direction of either your "Yes" or your "No" direction.

❧ When choosing a pendulum you can ask, "Is this a good pendulum for me to work with?" Hopefully you will get a "Yes." Otherwise try another pendulum or try asking again later.

❧ When starting a session and asking questions to your pendulum, start by confirming, "Do I have a spirit from the white light that is working with me through this pendulum?"

❧ You may use your pendulum during an animal communication session to ask yes or no questions about your animal's health or other concerns. You can also use your pendulum over a map when you are trying to find a lost animal.

❧ If you are having difficulty, such as the pendulum bobbing up and down, but not going in a particular direction, try changing the wording of your question to be more specific.

�**᛭** You can overdo the yes or no pendulum questions by continuing to ask in different ways until you get the answer you want. At this point you will not get accurate answers. Also, if you are too emotionally involved in the answer, this may affect the accuracy. In this case you may want to have another person ask the questions. Alternatively, you can write the possible answers on pieces of paper, turn the papers facedown, and mix them up. Then ask your pendulum, "Is this the answer?"

To Detect Energy Imbalances

☙ I find that a pendulum is most reliable for determining health issues or energy imbalances.

☙ Always protect yourself with Divine white light as you would with any connection to Spirit.

☙ Hold the pendulum over each of your animal's chakras. You may do this in turn, starting at the Crown Chakra and moving down to the Base Chakra. Place the pendulum about four inches above the top of the head. For the other chakras, hold the pendulum about two inches above their body. For the Base Chakra, you do not want to place the pendulum between their legs. Place the pendulum about four to six inches above their tail. Have the intention that the pendulum will pick up on the energy of the Base Chakra.

☙ You do not need to check all of the chakras in order. You can simply check one chakra if you feel you need some guidance on the energy of that chakra.

☙ The pendulum acts like a magnet, showing the electric field of the chakra and will rotate at the same speed and direction as the chakra. If it is slow, it means that the chakra is slow or slightly shutdown. If it is stopped, the chakra is completely shutdown. If it bounces up and down or is choppy, this is an energy imbalance. Applying healing energy should clear and open the chakra and then you can retest it. A healthy chakra should rotate at an even energetic pace, smoothly in one direction.

❧ After checking the chakras down their back, recheck on their front. (Chakras open at the front and back.)

❧ The direction of the chakra is individual to each animal. Some chakras rotate clockwise, others rotate counterclockwise, and some have a mixture of the two (meaning some of their chakras rotate one direction while others in the opposite direction). As long as they are rotating smoothly and with good speed, they are perfectly healthy.

❧ The pendulum is not healing or in any way affecting the energy imbalances. It simply acts as a guide to tell you where to direct your energy.

Note:

If you are having difficulty getting a clear YES/NO or finding the chakra, make sure you have asked for protection and have confirmed that a spirit from the white light is working with you. You can also cleanse your pendulum by burning sage and letting the smoke run over it or placing the pendulum in a bowl of water with sea salt.

About the Author

Gail Thackray was raised in Yorkshire, England and prides herself on having kept her English down-to-earth sensibility. Her life changed at age forty when she discovered she was a medium and able to talk to spirits on the other side, as well as animals. Helping others connect to Source and to develop their own natural psychic abilities is her passion. Gail lectures at events worldwide, doing live appearances as a healer, medium, and animal communicator. When at home in Los Angeles, she writes, lectures, and teaches about mediumship, healing, animal communication, manifesting, and other aspects of spirituality.

To learn more about Gail, please visit her website:
www.GailThackray.com

Notes

CPSIA information can be obtained
at www.ICGtesting.com
Printed in the USA
EDOW022047250213
737ED